FATHERS
AND
CUSTODY

BY WIN ANN WINKLER:

Post Mastectomy

FATHERS
AND
CUSTODY

Ira Victor and
Win Ann Winkler

HAWTHORN BOOKS, INC.
PUBLISHERS/New York

Material reprinted from an article entitled "Joint Custody: Is Sharing the Child a Dangerous Idea?" by Georgia Dullea copyright © 1976 by The New York Times Company. Reprinted by permission.

Material reprinted from an article entitled "Should You Accept Alimony?" by Betty Friedan copyright © 1976 The Hearst Corporation. Reprinted by permission of *Harper's Bazaar*.

Material reprinted from an article entitled "How Divorce Really Affects Children: A Major Report," by Shirley Streshinsky copyright © 1976 by The Redbook Publishing Company. Reprinted from *Redbook* magazine.

Material reprinted from *Fathering*, by Maureen Green, is copyright © 1976 by Maureen Green and is used here with permission of McGraw-Hill Book Company.

FATHERS AND CUSTODY

Library of Congress Catalog Card Number: 76–24224
ISBN: 0–8015–2560–8
 2 3 4 5 6 7 8 9 10

TO ALL OUR CHILDREN

CONTENTS

87238

Contents

ACKNOWLEDGMENTS

We would like to thank the mothers, fathers, and children who made us part of their homes in the preparation of this book. We would like especially to thank Dr. Harry Finkelstein Keshet of Brandeis University and Judith Wallerstein of the University of California at Berkeley for sharing their research with us. We appreciate the concern of the divorced mothers who helped us gain a clearer perspective on the scope of the problem. Roy Young of Divorced Men of Connecticut was invaluable to us in keeping us advised of activity in the divorced fathers' movement. Dixie deVienne of Stepparents Forum was invaluable to us with her insight and understanding of the step situation. We owe a special word of thanks to the children whose unsolicited comments gave us an insight into the lives of children of divorce not usually found in the theories of scholars and academicians. And to our editor, Sandra Choron, our special thanks for her patience with all our revisions and the time extensions needed for expanding our original outline on the book. It is traditional among writers to gratefully acknowledge the essential support of faithful devotees who type the manuscript and bring them unending cups of coffee. For this the authors thank each other.

INTRODUCTION

Who is the custodial father? Who is the father fighting for custody? What effect does a father-headed household have on the upbringing of children? Who is the joint-custodial father? How do his children manage living in two households? Above all, how is the custodial father managing sole responsibility for the upbringing of his children? What kind of a "single parent" is he? How are children affected by a motherless household?

These are the questions we asked ourselves when we undertook the writing of this book. Ira is a divorced father who has made some progress in his attempts to obtain custody of his two children. As co-director of the Family Law Counsel, for three years he has been helping other divorced fathers to gain such minor victories as being able to get mail delivered to their children through the schools (and being overruled by the postmaster general). Win is unmarried and childless and has, on more than one occasion, unwittingly been used as a weapon in unresolved postdivorce conflict involving children.

When we started on this project, we thought we would come up with a composite picture of the custodial father, who would conveniently pigeonhole himself into a comfortable little niche, according to our prearranged concepts. We had hoped to come up with a fully identifiable and recognizable average father. We had hoped to draw pat conclusions and even suggest lists of household chores to be pinned up on the kitchen wall as to how the custodial father could manage.

We had to face a rude awakening. The custodial or would-be

custodial father was simply not fitting into our pat little image. There were college professors, doctors, lawyers, blue-collar workers, farmers, schoolteachers, and, of course, the state of the economy being what it is, quite a few unemployed. We spoke to members of minority groups as well as those in the mainstream of American society. Among the noncustodial fathers, we learned of the inner workings of "visitation roulette" and "courtroom roulette," whereby a man's relationship with his children can be totally and irrevocably destroyed with the full approval or studiously averted glances of the law.

Our method of collecting data was slightly unorthodox. Hundreds of fathers all across the country were, of course, contacted. In most cases we went into the homes of the partly custodial and full-custodial fathers. We spoke to men at divorced fathers' group meetings. We had telephone conversations with other fathers who were referred to us when they heard of our project. Quite a few men refused to speak to us. In these cases, we got the outline of the situation from cooperating fathers, who explained to us that the subject was still too painful for their friends to discuss with outsiders. At no time did we send questionnaires to anyone. We simply could not use a clinical, bureaucratic approach to questions that required gut answers. During one interview, Ira was called upon to change the diaper of a three-year-old who decided to "break training" at our appearance. Win got roped into a dog-washing session at another home. Ira had to conduct one interview during a game of touch football. Win got thrown out of her office by a four-year-old who accompanied his father to the interview and decided that *he* wanted to write a book instead—on Win's typewriter.

Our discussions were not limited to fathers. We spoke to mothers, stepmothers, and women involved with divorced fathers. We spoke to lawyers and psychologists, some of whom underwent radical changes in their views on the child custody picture when they themselves became divorced.

The national divorce rate is approaching one in two. States that have adopted no-fault divorce laws surpass that figure. Traditionally, divorce proceedings have come under the adversary system in courts of law, and even in "no-fault" divorce settlements, children are regarded as more of a property settlement than human beings. Court practice of automatically awarding custody to the mother has been in effect since the beginning of the century. The father, it was assumed, either did not want custody, was unable to cope with it, deserved to be punished, or a combination of all three.

We can no longer close our eyes to the devastation caused by the shattered father–child relationship, which is a direct result of the custody-visitation practices that currently prevail, and which reduce the noncustodial parent to cipher status. We will have to replace our clichés about men being constitutionally unfit to raise children with the overwhelming evidence that there are men who are functioning competently in this role.

The myth of divorced mother as wronged victim and divorced father as brutish cad still prevails, although the stigma of divorce itself has lessened somewhat. It is not our intention to create role reversal in prejudice or discrimination. We do not believe that the stated desire for child custody confers sainthood or competence on mothers or fathers.

We are, however, trying to present as complete and objective a picture as possible of the growing number of men who are fighting for custody of their children—or, at least, for the right to play some meaningful roles in their children's lives—and the uphill battles they must face against legal, societal, and cultural prejudices.

We owe it to our children. And whether or not we have children, we owe it to society.

FATHERS
AND
CUSTODY

1
BREAKFAST

KEN

"How come you're not having any toast?" Ken H., a social studies teacher, asks his seventeen-year-old daughter, Ellen.

"I'm on a diet, Dad."

He shakes his head, trying to hide a smile, as Ellen carefully spoons some cottage cheese onto her plate.

"You'll take the meat out of the freezer when you get home from school, won't you?" he asks.

Ellen shakes her head slowly as she contemplates the cottage cheese. "I don't know, Dad. I may stay for a math tutoring class."

"You're pretty serious about this engineering thing, aren't you?"

"I want to at least give it a try," Ellen answers.

More small talk is exchanged between Ken and Ellen. During the two years he has had full custody of Ellen, he has learned that most of his apprehensions have been unfounded. Not that he had worried about the logistics of housework. He had shared an apartment with three other men during college and had done most of the housework and cooking during his sixteen-year marriage to Florence. Ellen was doing well in school and she certainly didn't lack for friends her own age. The marijuana incident had him worried for a while, but Ellen seemed to have handled it well. After all, quite a few of his students had told him about their experiments with pot, and he had concluded that it was just that—an experiment. Ellen told him that all her friends had tried it a couple of times and let it go at that. None of her friends was into the "hard stuff," she had told him, and he believed her. Ken had a way with kids. As one of his students had said to him,

"You know, Ken, we all have a hard time having to call you mister in class.

He and Ellen eat in silence for a while.

"Dad," Ellen says, "I'm worried about Brian."

"We've been through this before," he answers. "At this age, maybe it's better for Brian to be with his mother, and besides, maybe the experience of living in a big city will be good for him. As Mom's job demands more of her time, she'll probably be happy to give Brian back to us. We'll just have to learn to be patient."

"But, Dad," Ellen continues. "Brian was only four when Mom took him. Now he's six. We only see him on Christmas and Easter, and I'm worried about how he's growing up."

"Remember," Ken says, trying to reassure her, "Mom brought you up, too. I don't think she's beating Brian."

Ellen sets her lips in a hard line.

"I'm not talking about child abuse, Dad. But you know as well as I do, if Brian spends any more time with Mom, all he'll learn to do is sit in a corner, be quiet, and read a book."

Ken sighs and looks out the window.

CHUCK

The sun streams through the kitchen window of Chuck's painstakingly restored eighteenth-century stone farmhouse. He has gotten a late start this morning. Chuck, Jr., eight, dawdles over dressing, and Margaret, five, for no apparent reason, announces that she doesn't want to go to the baby-sitter's after school.

"OK, OK, finish your juice before you start on the chocolate milk."

"I want whipped cream on my Rice Krispies," announces Chuck, Jr.

"You don't get whipped cream on Rice Krispies," answers Chuck.

"Then I want chocolate syrup," answers his son.

"Come on, son," says Chuck. "Summer's coming up and you don't want any extra weight on you for swimming, do you? Remember how we talked that this summer you're going to start swimming without the tube?"

"I want chocolate syrup *and* whipped cream on my Rice Krispies," answers the boy, banging his spoon against the table.

Chuck looks down at his own plate. Chuck, Jr., has been eating compulsively during the past year. His weight is getting to the point where the other kids are calling him Butterball.

4

"Eat your Rice Krispies," he says to Margaret.

"I don't want Rice Krispies," she answers. "I want my chocolate milk."

"Drink your chocolate milk, then," Chuck answers her.

"I don't want my chocolate milk like *that*," she says.

"Then how *do* you want your chocolate milk?" he asks, trying to keep the edge of anger out of his voice.

Margaret slumps in her chair and looks at him defiantly.

"I want my chocolate milk in a *bottle*," she declares.

Rage creeps up on Chuck before he is aware what is happening.

"A *bottle*," he explodes. "A *bottle*! Bottles are for babies. You're a big girl. You're in kindergarten. You had a birthday last month and you were five, remember? Five years old! Five isn't a baby anymore."

The child slumps deeper into her chair. Thumb in her mouth, she whimpers, "I want my chocolate milk in a *bottle*."

Chuck goes through the motions of clearing the table. His worst fears had not materialized. There had been no nightmares or tantrums from either of the children. When he told them, just a year ago, that their mother had gone away that morning and wouldn't be back, Margaret had continued playing with the cat. Chuck, Jr., had looked up from the television set and answered, "Oh. She's never home anyway."

Sure, the boy's school work had taken a nose dive, but you have to expect some problems, don't you? The baby-sitter who called for the children after school and kept them until Chuck picked them up after work loved children. She had three of her own and took care of two others from single-parent, working homes. She was licensed by the county, and as everyone agreed, Mrs. Rigney had a way with children.

It was Margaret that Chuck had worried about most. After all, she had just turned four when his wife walked out. She really was a baby, he thought, feeling guilty about blowing up over the bottle incident. She needed a mother.

"No trouble at all," Mrs. Rigney had assured him. Just sits in a corner like a little lamb. A perfect little lamb. Not like some of the terrors I've got," and she laughed.

Chuck prided himself on how he had managed during the past year. The housework did get done, even if there was some dust in the corners. He planned meals in advance and the kids weren't fussy eaters—usually. What he had worried about—shopping for clothes for Margaret—turned out to be easier than he had expected. There

5

was a little children's shop in town, and the saleswoman there was very helpful.

Did he dare breathe a sigh of relief? Only recently had he begun sleeping nights again and not keeping one ear open for possible nightmares. That was a good sign, certainly. No nightmares, no tantrums.

But, still, Chuck had that uneasy feeling—*something wasn't right.*

PETE

"Dad, can we have pancakes for breakfast?" asks ten-year-old Denny.

"No, dope," answers his brother, Billy, with the profound wisdom of a twelve-year-old. "Today's a school day and we can only have pancakes when there's no school."

Tim, fourteen, is the oldest of Pete's three sons and is used to taking charge. He settles the dispute in his own way.

"Denny, get your erector set off the table so we can all have a place to eat."

Pete sits down in the nearest available chair with his three sons.

"OK, gang, knock it off. There's something we have to talk about."

Billy goes to the closet to get the peanut butter and returns to the table.

"Do you know what food prices are like?" Pete asks his three sons.

"High," answers Tim.

"But we raise our own cattle, Daddy, so we don't have to spend as much money for food as other people," Denny starts.

"But we have to eat other things besides, dope," answers Billy, attacking the peanut butter jar with a vengeance.

Pete disregards the bickering of the two younger boys.

"You know that camping trip to Canada we're planning for," he continues. "We're OK on tents and sleeping bags, but there are traveling expenses and side trips. Food prices are out of sight, so we're going to have to start a vegetable garden and follow it through. We've got the soil and we've got the equipment."

"Remember we started one last year, Daddy?" asks Denny.

"This year isn't last year," Pete answers. "This year we follow it through. Make it work. All of us."

Breakfast—consisting of peanut butter, orange juice, toast, dry cereal, and more peanut butter—follows. The boys get up to leave for school.

"Hey," yells Pete. "Who's doing the dishes?"

"Later, Dad, when we get home from school," answers Billy.

Pete gets up from the table and puts his jacket on. He has had full custody of the boys for eight years and is past the point where un-washed dishes bother him. It was agreed when he and Marge split that the boys would stay with him. Marge had wanted things that he couldn't give her, and when she met someone who could, he didn't stop her. She came to see the kids a couple of times a year. They really got a big kick out of the Mercedes, and besides, she would buy them all those things. Tim, the oldest, took it the hardest when she left, but they all went to that family counselor the school suggested—Marge, too—and things had worked out all right. His family operated as a team, and that was all he cared about. Sure, plenty of women had tried to lay the trip on him about how the boys needed a mother. Teachers and neighbors all kept a special eye out for the kids. He could go to the plant where he worked in the maintenance depart-ment every day and not worry. The boys could always reach him. Neighbors had left their phone numbers for the boys to use in case of emergency.

He hadn't understood what the assistant principal, a quiet-spoken woman in her mid-fifties meant when she said, "There's something golden about your sons."

They operated as a team. They all pulled together. That's all Pete cared about.

JAKE

The kitchen in Jake's house could be featured in *House Beautiful*. Coordinated cabinets and appliances, hanging utensils gleaming just enough not to look clinical—it comes as no surprise to learn that Jake, forty-two, is design director of a large architectural firm. Jake has had custody of Ted, fifteen, and Alison and Kimberly, the thirteen-year-old twins, for two years now.

"It's Saturday," Jake announces, as he clambers on the stool of the breakfast bar, "and we divvy up the chores." With that statement, he produces the mimeographed form with the list of household chores to be done throughout the week, a blank space after each for the members to fill in his or her name.

"I can't stand bathrooms, Dad," says Ted. "I'll take the lawn and the leaves if someone will help me stuff them into the plastic bags."

"I don't mind the bathrooms. I'll take them," announces Alison.

"You've been doing all indoor work for a couple of months now, Alison," Jake answers. "How about helping Ted with some of the raking and letting him do the small bathroom downstairs?"

"Yuk," answers Ted. "I'll do all the laundry besides the yard, but *not* that yukky bathroom."

"All the more reason to do that yukky bathroom," answers Jake. "Besides, Kimberly is down for the laundry."

"But as long as Ted offered to do the laundry," chimes in Kimberly, "I wanted to rehearse all week for tryouts for the school play. And," appealing to Ted, "if you do the laundry this week, I'll do the leaf-raking scene for you next week."

"Easy on the trade-offs and put-offs," Jake answers. "We'll do what we can to make the laundry loads easier for you, but rehearsing doesn't take all that time."

He tries to sound authoritative, but inwardly Jake's heart leaps. When he had taken full custody of the kids, Kimberly had been the shyest of all. When he asked her why she didn't have friends over to the house, she had answered, "Because I have no friends." Now he could hardly keep up with the kids' schedules. How do you simultaneously attend a hockey game in which your kid is playing, take another one to ballet class, and sit down and go over the sketches the third has done planning to redecorate her room? Alison is interested in interior design, and she has the stick-to-itiveness necessary to follow through on detail.

He shoos Mulligatawny, the Irish setter, away from the table. How do you prevent yourself from feeling smug? For a moment his brow clouds over. How would Elizabeth fit into this whole setup? Sure, the girls took to her, but Ted had his reservations.

"She's not my mother and she never will be," he had announced.

"No one's asking her to be your mother," Jake had tried to explain. "She's the woman I'm planning on marrying. That means we're going to have to set up a new home, a home that will meet the needs of six people, not five. There are going to be changes for all of us. It's a challenge that we all have to face together."

But Jake wondered about Elizabeth. She had no children of her own. She was devoted to her career and had just been promoted to top management. Their joint income would take a lot of pressure off him. Especially when the kids started college. Besides, after they were married, they would be able to afford full-time household help. No more hassling at the office about whether the meat got taken out of the freezer on time.

He and Elizabeth had discussed it. She made no pretenses about living happily ever after. She was aware that there would be problems and she was ready to face them. Elizabeth was accustomed to facing problems. She had to be to become director of marketing in a male-dominated industry. Still, he wondered.

Ted breaks in on his musing. "What time is dinner tonight, Dad?"

"A little later," he adds. "Elizabeth is coming over, and we'd like to have a quiet drink together before dinner."

"How come you two can start drinking and it's perfectly all right, but when other people take a drink suddenly they have to be put away somewhere." There is anger and defiance in Ted's voice.

"I've explained before, Ted," Jake tries to be patient. "There's a difference between two people having an occasional drink together for relaxation and people drinking constantly so that it becomes a sickness and then they're not able to function properly."

Ted is silent but continues to glare at Jake.

Jake realizes that there is still a price the children will have to pay for having lived in the custody of an alcoholic mother.

ED

Ed and Helen have what is called a reconstituted family. Ed's son, eleven-year-old Mark, and Helen's two daughters, Chris, ten, and Louise, seven, live with them. Ed's first wife, Dorothy, has custody of Scott, Ed's eight-year-old son. Scott spends alternate weekends with Ed and Helen, referring to their household as "my big family." Ed is a lawyer, Helen is a lab assistant at a major teaching hospital. On this particular morning, the four kids have scrambled out to play, leaving Ed and Helen alone at the table. Ed sees the look in Helen's eyes and silently thinks, "Here we go again."

"Scott is a different child when he's with us," Helen begins. "Can't you see that?"

"Must we go through this again?" answers Ed. "Scott has his life with Dorothy and her husband. He seems to get along well with Richard. He has friends, and he's doing well in school."

Helen's eyes are blazing now. "Can't you hear what Scott *doesn't* say? Dorothy has been institutionalized four times in the last eight years. Scott belongs here, Ed. *With us.*"

Ed gets up and paces around the room. One of his courtroom scenes comes back to haunt him: He had represented and won custody for a proven drug-addicted mother in a bitterly contested suit.

ELY

"OK, kids. Let's get this table in the middle of the room. Lisa, get the juice out of the refrigerator. Tanya, put the bread in the toaster."

"Daddy, if we leave our sleeping bags here can we come and live with you every weekend?"

Eli has been fighting for custody of his daughters, Lisa, ten, and Tanya, seven, for three years. During those three years he has fought and lost minor points. And some major ones. Not being consulted, for example, when Tanya had her tonsils out, although he was on the administrative staff of a teaching hospital and knew about the controversy surrounding tonsillectomies in children; not being able to consult with a teacher when Lisa unexplainedly dropped out of the school orchestra. And, of course, the overnight visitation, absolutely overruled by the judge. Ely moved into a studio apartment following the divorce. Two *girls* sleeping in the same room with their father?

Fortunately, Marsha, Ely's former wife, had met a man who began inviting her on weekend trips, and then announced to Ely that she was "dropping the girls off" at his place for the weekend. It meant that he suddenly had to cancel his date with Andrea, who let him know in no uncertain terms that his first wife had him "where the hair was pretty short." He wasn't worried about explanations to Andrea at this moment. How was he going to explain to the girls that his function as a father was contingent upon the crumbs thrown from their mother's table? How could he explain justice to a child who was just starting social studies in school. In short, how could he be a father in more than name only?

Ely had just joined a divorced fathers' group in his city. Maybe he could talk it over with some of the other men there who were grappling with the same problems.

LARRY

Larry hurriedly sets the breakfast table for himself and his children, Deborah, nine, and Michael, six. Does he have the right breakfast cereal? They say something about how kids are supposed to have hot cereal in the morning and he doesn't know how to make oatmeal. What about milk? Should he have gotten regular homogenized instead of the slim-trim fat-free stuff he always keeps for himself? What about orange juice? Maybe the kids should have fresh orange juice. He tries to calm himself. His friends, the Friedlanders, were going to England and maybe he could get Mrs. Andrews, their housekeeper. It had all happened so suddenly. If he had only had time at least to plan. For Chrissake, to plan.

"Is everything all right?" he asks anxiously as the children sit down at the table. "I mean is this kind of breakfast cereal OK? They have it on television. I mean, this is the kind kids like, isn't it? Or do you usually have oatmeal? We can have oatmeal, you know, when we get more settled."

"I hate oatmeal, Daddy," announces Deborah.

"Oatmeal is *yeeech*," declares Michael solemnly. I mean really *yeeech*."

Larry breathes a momentary sigh of relief. Maybe it wouldn't be so bad after all. He'd work things out, step by step. Just like at the office where he is in charge of a structural engineering project. Slowly, step by step. One thing at a time. And it's all a matter of planning.

"Daddy," starts Deborah, "are we going to live with you always?"

"And can they send my bicycle and my hamster here?" adds Michael.

How could he answer them? It had been five years since the divorce, and he had seen the children only twice a year when he flew to Chicago for Christmas and Easter. Sure, he had thought about custody at the time of the divorce, but his lawyer had only laughed at him.

"This way you're only giving up the house and the kids, Larry. Get into a custody battle and it will cost you your career and chance for a future life as well."

Sure, Roberta had cracked up during her second marriage, but her mother had flown out to help with the kids. Now her mother was living in Florida and had recently broken her hip. With Roberta's third marriage falling apart, she simply had called Larry collect to announce, "You've got to take the children. I simply can't cope."

What were his chances of getting custody now? Roberta could possibly emerge from the mental institution held together with tranquilizers and clichés while her lawyer put a verbal halo around her with his tirade about her having discovered that her true vocation is motherhood.

RALPH

Ralph, a free-lance illustrator, sits down to breakfast in his loft.

"We have a new kind of jam today, Dad," his son, Eric, states proudly. Eric is nine. Ralph has had custody of Eric since he was three. No custody battle there. His wife, Natalie, simply announced that she had had it with the kid number and she was splitting to get into little theater work.

Ralph studies the jar of jam carefully. "It looks terrific, Eric. And I bet it will be really good with this toast, too."

That was part of their division of labor. Eric is responsible for breakfast, Ralph for dinner. He has managed fairly well with Eric with the help of nursery schools, baby-sitters, neighbors, and family. Fortunately, he is able to work out of his large living loft, and clients have been pretty understanding about sudden changes in appointments. Weekends are beginning to present a problem, though, because Ralph has been getting into mountain climbing and feels he is ready to start on some overnight trips.

"Do you think she'll like me, Dad?" Eric interrupts as Ralph is musing through the L. L. Bean catalog.

"Who?" asks Ralph, looking up suddenly.

"Her. You know, I mean, my mother."

"I don't see why not," Ralph answers. "Everyone else does."

Ralph was at least as apprehensive about the meeting between Natalie and Eric as the boy was. For five years she had refused to have anything to do with Eric, but last year she had agreed to talk with him on the phone. Maybe she could sort of get it together with that new marriage. Maybe she and Eric could sort of hit it off together. After all, he wasn't a baby anymore, so she wouldn't have to give him the physical care. Maybe all those different encounter trips—Zen, TM, est, bioenergetics—had helped her in some way. Now she was into a new thing where they submerge you into a bathtub. The whole kit and kaboodle.

Maybe things would get to the point where Natalie would even consider taking Eric for a weekend sometimes.

Maybe he could really get into that climbing scene!

GLADSTONE

Gladstone sits at his kitchen table with a cup of instant coffee and a mountain of paper work that threatens to become an avalanche. Since he decided to fight *pro se* for Melissa, his head has been a whirlwind of legal terminology, but he has no funds left for any more lawyers. First there was family court and all those delays and overrulings. Gladstone had asked for the weekend shift at the hospital where he worked so that he could keep weekdays free for Melissa, whose mother was a schoolteacher and who was currently being cared for by a series of baby-sitters. He still lived in the apartment they all had shared when they were together. He transfers a pile of papers onto the high chair.

Is it worth it? Does he have any chance against the system? He tries to put those thoughts out of his mind. He has to think he has a chance. It is the only way he can keep going. He had tried to reason with Virginia, his former wife. Certainly she knew how important it was for Melissa's development to have a sense of security with two parents. Virginia would have known that from her teacher training days. Early child psychology and all that.

Would anyone listen? What chance did a black man have in the courts anyway?

Gladstone takes his coffee and goes into the living room. As he sits down in the upholstered chair something seems to be poking him in the back. He reaches around to remove it.

It is Melissa's teddy bear.

MATTHEW

Matthew is proud of the breakfast table Lois has set. It is the first time the children, Judy, twelve, and Tom, nine, have slept over. Sure, it was no secret that Matthew had been living with Lois for over a year; it was just the sort of thing that had never been openly mentioned. He was apprehensive about what kind of tales the children would take back to Ramona, his former wife. What about Lois? Would she be resentful about the children spending too many weekends with them? How would he effect the transition from five-hours-on-Sunday father to weekend father? The kids seemed right at home there, though. Judy was into Lois's ballet books and Tom was busy with the chess set, trying to memorize the moves of the bishop and the rook. Not like before, the constant shuffling between the zoo and museum and a bunch of movies Matthew never wanted to see.

"Where did you get this pretty sugar bowl?" Judy asks Lois.

Matthew beams. "Is everything going OK, kids?"

Tom answers, "This is the best breakfast we ever had, Ronald."

Ronald is the name of Ramona's lover, who had moved in with her and the children on the day Matthew moved out, three years ago.

CLINT

Breakfast is a fairly routine matter at Clint's home. He sets the table the night before so that he and the kids, Carol, nine, and Deren, seven, can talk about their plans for the day without the hassle of setting the table.

"Where's my special glass?" Deren asks him. "You know, with Batman on it."

Clint wonders what it is that he has forgotten. He doesn't remember anything about a Batman glass.

"No, not here, Deren," answers Carol. That's at Mommy's. The Batman glass is at Mommy's house."

"Oh, I forgot," exclaims Deren.

Clint and his ex-wife, Nina, have joint custody of the children, by their decision, not the judges' and lawyers'. Their two apartments are four blocks apart, with the children's school midway between the two homes. The children spend a week with each parent. Clint and Nina's arrangement has been cited by their about-to-be-divorced friends as a model setup. Vacation and holiday plans are always discussed in advance with the children present. There is openness and flexibility in visitation, and decisions about the children, medical care, and vacations are decided upon jointly. Clint and Nina both feel that their lives have improved since the divorce. Clint is a free-lance editor and Nina a nursery school teacher. They have adjusted their respective work schedules to allow for more time with the children. Their incomes are about equal, so there has never been a financial hassle.

Clint and Nina are unusual in one other crucial aspect: Each feels that the other has something unique to offer to the children, each respects the parental abilities of the other, and each speaks highly of the other, both to the children and to outsiders.

They have had joint custody for three years now. Both Clint and Nina admit to anxieties in the early stages of the arrangement. Would the children express a preference for one parent over the other? Would one try to win the children away from the other? Time and openness have allayed these anxieties. The children feel they are wanted in two homes. In fact, it has been remarked on more than one occasion that Clint's and Nina's trust, respect, and admiration for one another's parental abilities is deeper than is found in most two-parent homes.

Unfortunately, their situation is not typical.

BEN

Ben is no stranger to housekeeping chores when his children, Hilary, nine, and Jeffrey, seven, come to spend a week with him during school holidays. He had been fully domesticated during his marriage to Sarah, who was heavily involved with the feminist movement. Unfortunately, her interest never reached the stage where she was able to develop herself into a career position. Rather, it became deadlocked into resentment at the housewife role and antagonism toward men.

When the separation was decided upon, Sarah announced that they would base their custody arrangements on the model of Clint and Nina. Although it worked out for a while, Sarah could not really cope with independence and moved back into her parents' home five hundred miles away, taking the children with her. Ben, in the meantime, had grown strongly attached to the children. True, visitation was such that he could visit the children whenever he wanted, but whenever he wanted was not whenever he could afford it. Ben pleaded with Sarah. Even during the marriage he had been the "domestic" in addition to being the "breadwinner." Sarah had answered him with all the rhetoric she could muster: "The divorce will have a maturing effect on the children and help them cope with reality in their later lives."

Ben has to concede on this particular morning that the small country town where the children are living is better for them than the city upbringing they would have gotten had he fought for and obtained custody of them. Hilary and Jeffrey are bubbling over with tales of newfound friends, hayrides, and playing on streets "where they don't chase you away."

Jeffrey, his appetite whetted by clean country air, reaches for another piece of bread and honey.

"Dad, why can't you move to the country, too, so it can be like before?"

Ben tries to go over the speeches he has rehearsed so many times. How Daddy had to work in the city. How just because Mommy and Daddy were divorced, it didn't mean they didn't both love the children. How Daddy always cared about them both even if he couldn't see them as much as they'd all like.

Suddenly, Hilary interrupts him.

"I *hate* it," she cries. "I *hate* divorce. I wish there were a law against divorce."

Feebly, Ben tries to pull out the arguments with which Sarah had coached him so dutifully.

"But when two grown-up people don't love each other any more it's really the best thing for them not to live together. Of course, you both may have feelings of anger and hurt but you have to realize that it's the best thing."

Hilary hurls the bowl of cereal across the kitchen.

"I *hate* it," she shrieks.

"Because it means that kids can't see their fathers any more," Jeffrey adds.

Ben pushes his plate of bacon and eggs away and buries his head in his arms. He always prided himself on the fact that he never cried in front of the children.

2

FED UP

A bit of joy; my boys called me last night. Surreptitously, of course, but we had a good conversation. I hope that it doesn't have to do me another year and a half.

The above is an excerpt from a letter we received from Art, a father whose case we have been following for two years. Art is a father who is fed up. He is not alone. As the divorce rate races toward 1 in 2.5 marriages and as more than one million children join the ranks of children of divorce each year, more and more fathers are questioning the status quo and the second-class-parent rank conferred upon them.

More fathers are fighting for full custody. More are fighting for joint or split custody (one or more children to each parent, depending upon the individual situation). Many more are fighting to have their visitation rights enforced. Like Art, they want something more than a surreptitious phone call every year and a half. Others are fighting because they feel that their visitation rights, when carried out according to the letter of the law, can destroy a father–child relationship far more effectively than a court order forbidding a father to have anything to do with his children. They are fed up with visitation rights that relegate them to the role of Sunday Santa, Disneyland Daddy, or Bozo the Clown.

One father, Paul, writes us that he was "very lucky" in maintaining his relationship with his son in spite of visitation obstacles:

Personally, I was very lucky with my oldest son who is now nineteen. I lost him when he was three, but he was definitely a father's boy and my ex-wife allowed me to see him whenever I wanted with minor restrictions. Many Sundays I went from Pennsylvania to Brooklyn to pick him up on a Sunday morning and then brought him back that night. We [Paul's second wife and their children] had a cohesive family with all four kids feeling like they belonged together.

Fathers are beginning to take action and that action takes many forms, not all of it beneficial to themselves or to their children, unfortunately. Child-snatching by both mothers and fathers is on the rise and is discussed fully later in this book. Divorced fathers' groups are mushrooming into what could loosely be called a movement. Like every movement it is split into factions: The extremist fringe speaks of bombing courthouses; the moderate faction is trying to work within the system, getting laws changed or enforced. Their prime goal is to see that the best interests of the children do not become the best interests of the lawyers. Many fathers are fighting to see that custody decisions are taken out of the hands of individual judges by appointment of panels of experts, which could include a psychologist or child behaviorist, a clergyman, a social worker, and a lawyer. Anthony Gil of the Family Law Counsel in New Jersey was divorced in 1971. Since then, he has been in court forty times trying to get his visitation rights enforced. Says Gil, "Matrimonial court is the judge's fiefdom; he has complete power over everything that occurs there." Carlo Basile, another member of Gil's group, has been in court seventy-six times in the past two years seeking visitation rights of his three sons.

Bitterness and resentment runs high among many fathers, and one can easily get the impression that many fathers are conducting private vendettas against the courts rather than being motivated by any desire to maintain a relationship with their children. One such father, Harold, feels that support payments ordered for the child of his first marriage are creating financial hardships for his second family. The story is not a pleasant one, and while we, frankly, cannot agree with Harold that his actions are motivated by altruistic concern for his older child, aspects of the situation do point out the manner in which a disgruntled first wife can attempt (sometimes successfully) to destroy a second marriage, aided and abetted by the legal system.

In brief, Harold's daughter, Arlette, is brain-damaged as the result of a birth injury, and while educable, will have to be cared for throughout her life. Harold and his first wife were in their early forties when Arlette was born. They divorced when Arlette was three. There were no visitation or financial problems, and Harold saw the child frequently. He was more a functioning than a visiting father; Arlette at the age of five still needed much of the care that young infants do. A bone of contention between Harold and his former wife was that while he felt Arlette needed special education (an opinion that received the support of various neurologists and child psychologists with whom he consulted), his former wife took the denial route with Arlette, insisting that she be placed in a regular kindergarten class. As the noncustodial parent, Harold was powerless to discuss the situation with school officials.

The problems really began when Harold married a woman half his age and their daughter, Nancy, was born a year later. Harold's second wife wanted Arlette to feel like a part of the family; as Nancy (a bright, alert child, to Harold's delight) grew up, she referred to Arlette as "my sister." Harold's first wife began using the tactics of "courtroom roulette," demanding increased support payments for Arlette. She had, by this time, conceded that Arlette did need special education and found a private school with tuition rates of $6,000 a year.

("Courtroom roulette" is a situation in which one party will drag the other into court on technicalities, designed primarily as a harrassment technique. Needless to say, a nonemployed person can jeopardize someone else's job by forcing courtroom appearances frequently.)

Harold's second wife appeared with him during one courtroom appearance. Nancy was then two. When Harold protested about doubled support payments in addition to the tuition for special schooling, the judge asked his wife, "Why don't you go to work and help him with the payments?" When she answered that she had a two-year-old child at home, the judge told her, "Go get a baby-sitter."

Harold, in the meantime, feels that his relationship with Arlette has been irrevocably destroyed. Because of her handicap, he feels that had things been otherwise, Arlette could have been integrated into his second family and her future would have been secure. When confronted with the choice of destroying either Arlette or his new family, he feels that "Arlette has already been destroyed."

Harold is fighting his battle alone. He has conferred with his local divorced fathers' group, but their opinion is that he is more interested in his private vendetta against the court system (which he feels is responsible for the destroyed relationship with Arlette) than in establishing any sort of responsible relationship with the child.

Bernard is another father who is fed up. During the two years he has been divorced, visitation has been carried out according to the letter of the law. His income provides for generous alimony and support payments for Caroline, his four-year-old daughter. He has never had any problem in calling for Caroline at eleven o'clock on Sunday mornings and returning her at six. His former wife has never resorted to the tactics of "visitation roulette" he hears about from so many of the other divorced fathers he knows.

(The term *visitation roulette*, often used in this book, has been popularly adopted among divorced sets and denotes the games divorced people play. Examples are cited throughout.)

One Saturday, Bernard's ex-wife called him and said she thought it would be better for Caroline not to go out the following day. When pressed for an explanation, his wife told him that during the past week Caroline had been rushed to the hospital; she had swallowed a quarter.

Bernard was enraged that he had not been notified. "I could have been supportive to her," he declared. "She needs a father at a time like that." Calmly, his former wife explained to him that indeed he could have been all these things, had Caroline only swallowed the quarter "on his time."

Furious, Bernard called the child's pediatrician, whom he knew personally, and demanded an explanation as to why he had not been notified. The explanation was simple: "You know what I would have let myself in for, Bernie. You're not the custodial parent."

He certainly did understand the doctor's position. He is a doctor himself.

Vincent had been fed up during his seven-year custody battle for his nine-year-old son, Joseph. In the beginning he had been fairly docile in accepting the court's decision that a working father was unable to provide a proper home for Joseph. He had hoped that his marriage to Rosemary, the child they had, and the small house they had just bought would convince the judge that they could provide a proper home for Joseph. Before marrying Rosemary, Vincent had made it clear to her that he hoped one day Joseph would be able to live with them. That was fine with Rosemary. The time Joseph had run away from his mother to come and stay with Vincent and Rosemary didn't have much effect on the judge—the police had taken Joseph away, threatening Vincent with "custodial interference" if Joseph were to come to them again.

Vincent had just about given up hope when it became necessary for Joseph's mother to be institutionalized. His lawyer told him that this was his big chance; it was extremely difficult to have a mother declared unfit. Vincent, a carpenter, worked nights and weekends to get Joseph's room ready.

Nevertheless, upon declaring the child's mother unfit, the court ordered Joseph to an institution that would eventually find him a foster home until his mother was completely rehabilitated.

Vincent is coming dangerously close to the end of his rope. He's found out about a few extremist groups who talk about bombing courthouses. Someone gave him a copy of a privately printed book entitled *The Rape of the Male*, whose cover depicts a crucifixion. It was written by Richard F. Doyle, who heads a group called Men's Rights Association, which puts out a newsletter entitled "The Liberator." Doyle's book opens with a chapter eloquently titled "View From the Bottom of the Toilet." His description of a case like Vincent's could well be summed up by the following:

> The average layman is conditioned to peace, to old-fashioned honesty and fair play, as incapable of fighting back as Little Bo Peep. He lies down and takes a screwing in court just to make some official think he's a good boy. He labors under the naïveté that he will avoid the rape simply by virtue of a pure heart. Bunk! A man like that is at a disadvantage more than at an advantage in this practical, everyday world; especially in court. The allegorical significance, if nothing else, of the crucifixion is undeniable. That's what happens to good guys.[1]

In his striped overalls, hammer and screwdriver in his pockets, it is difficult for Vincent to relate to most of the other men in the divorced fathers' group in his county. With their tailored suits, white-collar jobs, and talk about forming a caucus, lobbying for the ERA, and amalgamation with other groups, he feels alienated from these men who speak of "nurturing ability not limited to females." But he does

---

1. Richard F. Doyle, *The Rape of the Male* (St. Paul, Minn.: Poor Richard's Press, 1976), p. 168.

know that he and Joseph have always hit it off together OK, even though he had a hard time keeping the kid out of his toolbox when he was two. Vincent cannot understand how "those crazy women libbers with all their talk about men and women using the same toilets" can be the hope of the men in his group. As Vincent told Ira, "Just because some broad starts yakking about equal pay for equal work, do these guys think they're going to convince some judge who hasn't gotten it up in forty years that men can take care of their kids?"

Is it any wonder that Vincent feels a kinship with Doyle when he reads:

> The decline and fall of the male has been far too voluntary and justified—made so by the vast majority of near-normal males who have simply and quietly abdicated their own trousers. . . . The technically superior, white-collared men sabotage their sometimes more masculine blue-collared brothers. Many damaging propagandists are male writers pandering to the common bias.[2]

Charles Cornell is another father who got fed up. He and his wife were divorced in 1974. She remarried and moved to Jacksonville, taking the children with her.

"There was nothing I could do," he said. "You feel so helpless. You can say that they're your children too, but in almost all cases the mother gets the children and the father is demoted from parent to visitor."

Cornell did something about it, though. He got in touch with Doris Sassower, a New York City attorney known for her success in father-custody cases. Although Sassower was not able to handle the Cornell case directly, she did confer with his lawyer, and although Cornell lives in New York and his children in Florida, something of a joint-custody agreement was worked out. He is with his children "every summer 'as soon as school gets out until it starts again.' He can call them once a weekend and on holidays. Should the children decide they want to live with him permanently, they may do so by going before the judge and declaring their wishes. Cornell does not have to petition his ex-wife into court for such a proceeding."[3]

Cornell does not feel that he is unique as a father wanting to con-

2. Ibid., pp. 166–167.
3. "*Fathers Seek Right to Custody*," UPI, *Star-Ledger* (Corning, N.Y.), 4 July, 1976.

tinue his relationship with his children: "There are thousands of guys just like me right here in our own area," he says. "There are millions in the country. If they all got together and demanded their rights, just think of what might happen. Just think of it!"[4]

The decision in the Salk case in 1975 was hailed as a milestone by many custodial-hopeful fathers. The landmark aspect of this case was that Dr. Lee Salk, one of the better-known child psychologists, author and TV personality, had refused to bring the charge of "unfitness" against his wife, Kerstin:

> More important to professionals involved in family law— judges, lawyers and experts on child care—were two contemporary issues raised by the recent Salk decision, in which permanent custody of the children . . . was awarded to the father.
> The key issue is the rejection of the traditional presumption that a mother, unless "unfit" should get custody of a young child. This presumption lingers despite new laws in New York and elsewhere banning preference to either parent.[5]

Burton Monasch, president of the New York Chapter of the American Academy of Matrimonial Lawyers, says: ". . . it has been inexorable that you prove the mother unfit or that you leave the judge with at least a jaundiced view of her when you walk out of the courtroom."[6]

The Salk case also spotlighted another sensitive area in the custody question: that is, the children's preference, which, in this case, was to live with their father. While many people would take the view that the children's preference should be the determining factor in custody awards, armies of psychologists are equally ready to decry the notion that the children should become "burdened" with the decision.

Marvin is a father who is irate about the "fitness" tradition. Like so many other fathers, he doesn't feel he should have to prove his fitness for fatherhood in spite of being male. Nor does he feel that his wife is in any way an unfit mother. His two daughters, eight and eleven, get proper care and are clean and well-fed. He describes his former wife,

4. Ibid.
5. Georgia Dullea, "Who Gets Custody of Children? Fathers Now Are Being Heeded," *New York Times,* 14 October, 1975, p. 42.
6. Ibid.

an executive secretary in a major corporation, as intelligent and attractive.

"Frankly," he says, "I don't like my wife's friends. I don't like the values the girls are growing up with. They're learning to define people by the cars they drive. I'm concerned about their self-image as women and I don't like the attitude they're developing about man–woman relationships."

Marvin has been fighting for custody for five years.

"The guys who've got a clear-cut case of unfitness—you know, drugs, promiscuity—they've got it easy. Me, I've got to plead my case that no, I do not live in a garbage can, yes, I do know how to fry an egg, and with a little bit of tutoring I might even learn how to manage a washing machine."

Elliott, a custodial father of two girls, would laugh ruefully if he heard Marvin blithely talking about how easy it was to obtain custody on an "unfitness" charge. Sure, Gloria would get a little tight at parties before they split. Their friends were amused. "Gloria is just great once she lets go of those hang-ups," they would assure Elliott.

Originally, Elliott and Gloria had agreed on no-fault divorce, with Gloria keeping the kids. After they were separated for about six months, Elliott began hearing stories, but he was still paying for Gloria's analysis—she'd straighten out, all right. But there came a time when he returned the kids on Sunday night that he could no longer ignore the evidence—the house a shambles, calling out for a pizza for the kids' dinner. And the men—that whole battalion of "my new friend, a very sensitive and spiritual individual," picked up at a series of bars. She always felt she had to take them in, like stray cats.

One Sunday the girls just laid it on the line to him: "We don't want to go home, Daddy. She scares us." Just like that. Elliott realized he'd have to sue for custody, although his lawyer kept telling him he didn't stand a chance. Middle-class neighborhood, Gloria's Ph.D. in child psychology—no way. Elliott was determined to fight just the same.

After fifteen months of court proceedings, during which time Elliott had been investigated and declared fit (the judge kept ordering Gloria to "shape up and be a good mother"), Gloria turned up stoned in court. Custody was awarded to Elliott.

"Had I been the lush," he declares with a shake of the head, "it would have taken that judge exactly fifteen seconds to make his decision."

During that fifteen-month interim, Elliott had moved the girls—lock, stock, bicycles, and hamsters—into his four-room apartment, only to have to return them to Gloria under court order.

Frank and his second wife, Marion, are also fed up. Frank earns $25,000 a year as a sales executive. When Frank and his first wife divorced three years ago, she was awarded custody of their three children, a daughter, then aged eleven, and two sons, fourteen and sixteen. The boys, especially, wanted to live with Frank, who tried to explain to them that these things took time with the courts.

A year after the divorce, he met and married Marion, a divorcee with custody of her own two children, eight and ten. Marion earned $15,000 a year as a research assistant. When Frank's oldest son turned eighteen, he went to live with Frank, Marion, and her two children. The younger boy felt the loss of his brother very keenly, and on several occasions ran away to Frank's home, only to be returned by the police.

Frank went to court in an attempt to get his support payments modified, pointing out that the oldest boy had lived with him and the younger one planned on living with him as soon as he turned eighteen.

Frank certainly has his payment schedule modified. The judge awarded his first wife Frank's entire income on the basis that he, his older son (attending a local college), Marion, and her two children could live on Marion's salary.

The threat of prison for fathers who default on payments is a very real one. Roy Young, a divorced father from Connecticut, also got fed up with his situation. Here is Roy's story:

> Nine years after my marriage and after having twins of our own and after I adopted her daughter by a previous marriage, I kissed my wife goodbye in the morning and when I returned home from work that night my home was empty of kids, furniture, and feeling. Three days later I was served with papers and the war started. I finally found where they had moved, a mile away, and had a short chat with my twin boys. Over the next six months I saw my children a total of ninety-one minutes and then stopped paying the $250 per month child support.
>
> Hauled into court in April, November, December, and January, I adamantly refused to pay support unless the court enforced the other part of the judgment, which was my right to see

my children. The Connecticut State Supreme Court of Errors had already ruled that the requirement for a man to pay child support was completely unrelated to his right to see his children, so I was dead.

Early in January I was sentenced to an indeterminate term in the Litchfield Correctional Center. I was there until the end of March when the same judge released me without explanation. There was an investigation by the Family Relations Department, but in spite of ten years of stability, hard work, and a good income, I came out an ogre. No mention was made of the loose family background that she came from nor of the tightly knit family that I came from.

Heard at the hearing which jailed me were three motions: One, to have her found in contempt of court for ignoring the "reasonable rights of visitation" that I had been allowed; one for a reversal of custody based on the grounds that she was denying the children the sight and knowledge of their father; and the other for a jury trial.

All denied.

Extremely important was the fact that I was one of the founders and driving force behind the Divorced Men's Association of Connecticut. I still feel that the jail sentence was as a warning to other members.

It is now a year and a half later, and I haven't seen my children one minute in all that time. I had requested the school system to send my children's records to me, and that was refused at my wife's demand. I asked their pediatrician to let me know of any illness, but that, too, was refused.

The question must come to your mind as to why I don't just go over, twenty-three miles, and knock the doors down. Frankly, I have thought about it, but I feel that the kids will come around on their own and I can't subject them to the upheaval that this may cause. After all, they were almost eight years old when they lost their father, and their memories of me can't be erased.

I have not worked in over two years. I left a job paying over $25,000 because, what the hell, we only work for our family and I've decided to devote full time to this search for the Holy Grail. Money has run out, but even if I have to move to the "Y," I refuse to give in. Lately, it's been two days [a week] at court and at least two days of counseling. The growth of this group over the past month has been phenomenal.[7]

Most fathers fighting for custody would regard Greg as being one of the lucky ones. Greg got custody of four of his five children, and did not complain about having to pay his former wife child support for the fifth, even though she was working. He did, however, balk at paying her legal costs. The judge not only threatened him with jail, but said that the four children in his custody would be sent to an institution.

Some fathers, like Roy Young, are confident enough that their relationship with their children will not be jeopardized in spite of visitation denial and a jail sentence. Others, like Greg, will pay through the nose in order not to jeopardize what they've already won.

Others become desperate. Roy Young referred to "the question that must come to our mind." While Roy has flatly rejected "knocking the doors down" for fear of the upheaval it would cause the children, not every divorced father is as restrained as he is. Child-retrieval is rising at a rapid rate in proportion to the rise in no-fault divorce. This will be dealt with in detail in chapter 11.

These fathers, whether fighting for the right to be told of emergency medical situations regarding their children or the right to remove them from custody of an alcoholic mother, are fed up. They are fed up with a legal system that regards fatherhood as second-class parenthood in every area except financial support. They are fed up with the assumption that maleness automatically disqualifies them from parenthood. They are fed up with both visitation roulette and courtroom roulette. And they are taking action.

As noted earlier, not all of it is beneficial to themselves or their children.

7. Divorced Men of Connecticut, the fathers' group that Young heads, offers counseling to men going through this process.

3

THE EMERGENCE OF THE CUSTODIAL FATHER

Although there are no accurate statistics available on the number of divorced fathers with custody of their children, the table on the following page, taken from a Census Report of March 1975, is revealing. The top line indicates a 40.6 percent rise in female-headed households from 1970 to 1975. It is interesting to note that neither the table nor the report lists a heading for male-only households with own children. This is explained by the footnote: "Includes families with a male head, but no spouse present, not shown separately."

Given the table, we have to do some of our own mathematics in order to understand the trend in the rise of father-custody households. According to our deductions, there were 282,000 father-only families in a total of 10,853,000 (2.6 percent) in 1975, compared to 219,000 out of a total of 10,993,000 (2.0 percent) families in 1970. We have to bear in mind that this is the 35–44 age group only, with no breakdown of widowed, separated, and divorced men. Neither is there any breakdown of split custody, where one or more children live with each parent, nor of joint custody, where children divide their time between two homes. (See table on pages 30–31.)

Until recently, the divorced father had a clear-cut role and he usually followed it without kicking up his heels. Custody was awarded to the mother in more than 95 percent of all cases, and in the instances where the father was awarded custody, it was usually because the mother was not merely unable to cope with the demands of running a home and raising children but, more likely, was simply unable to function and had to be institutionalized for one reason or another.

The noncustodial father then had his choice of becoming law-abiding or law-breaking in his fatherhood role. On the surface, it would appear that if the father met support (and often, alimony) payments, he was law-abiding, but if he defaulted or was late in payments he was law-breaking. Actually, it was never quite as simple as that. In order for a divorced father to be a responsible citizen in the eyes of the law, he had to combine full financial responsibility for his children (often, in addition to his former wife) and step out of his children's lives in most other areas. Court-ordered visitation rights were contingent upon his wife's desire to see those visitation rights enforced, and then, as now, the quality as well as quantity of time with his children depended more on the whim of his former wife than on court orders. Then, as now, a father's insistence on having a say in the direction his children's lives were taking could bring the wrath of the courts upon him, in addition to having his visitation rights (but not financial responsibility) revoked.

It did not then, nor does it now, take very much to place a divorced father in the criminal category. Failure to meet either initially ordered payments or subsequent demands for increased payments, for whatever reason, can mean the threat of a jail sentence for a divorced father. Furthermore, unemployment and disability have not always released a father from his responsibility of regular support payments.

Who, then, is the custodial father? Why does a father fight for custody? How legion is his name? What problems does he face?

Regarding the full-custodial father, the simplest explanation is that he is the divorced man whose children live with him and whose wife has been awarded, and exercises, visitation rights, in a complete role reversal of traditional practice. At the other extreme, we visualize the stereotype of the visitation divorced father taking his children to a ball game or museum on Sunday, depending on his sociocultural bracket.

However, trends are changing in family structure and restructure, and as attitudes and controversies regarding divorce have undergone a complete upheaval, so are custodial practices undergoing upheaval, not all of them quiet. Role reversal in child custody cannot be defined merely as the father taking the children to live with him. Joint custody is being spotlighted, with experts pro and con sharpen-

FAMILIES WITH HEAD 35 TO 44 YEARS OLD BY TYPE, PRESENCE OF OWN CHILDREN UNDER 18 YEARS OLD,[1] AND BY SIZE: 1970 TO 1975

(NUMBERS IN THOUSANDS)

NUMBER OF OWN CHILDREN UNDER 18 AND SIZE OF FAMILY	1975			1970			PERCENT CHANGE, 1970 TO 1975		
	ALL FAMILIES[1]	HUSBAND-WIFE	FEMALE HEAD	ALL FAMILIES[1]	HUSBAND-WIFE	FEMALE HEAD	ALL FAMILIES[1]	HUSBAND-WIFE	FEMALE HEAD
Total families	10,853	9,060	1,511	10,993	9,699	1,075	-1.3	-6.6	40.6
Own Children Under 18									
No own children	1,318	986	211	1,287	1,026	154	2.4	-3.9	37.0
1 own child	2,029	1,579	394	1,828	1,533	252	11.0	3.0	56.3
2 own children	3,101	2,712	336	2,858	2,560	268	8.5	5.9	25.4
3 or more own children	4,406	3,784	570	5,020	4,581	400	-12.2	-17.4	42.5
Size of Family									
2 persons	1,206	695	391	1,132	745	267	6.5	-6.7	46.4
3 persons	1,723	1,282	363	1,559	1,258	264	10.5	1.9	37.5
4 persons	2,952	2,622	290	2,713	2,470	214	8.8	6.2	35.5
5 persons	2,456	2,240	196	2,468	2,312	145	-0.5	-3.1	35.2
6 persons	1,300	1,152	138	1,593	1,497	88	-18.4	-23.0	56.8
7 or more persons	1,216	1,069	134	1,527	1,417	97	-20.4	-24.6	38.1

PERCENT DISTRIBUTION

Total families.........	100.0	100.0	100.0	100.0	100.0	100.0	(x)	(x)	(x)
Own Children Under 18									
No own children	12.1	10.9	14.0	11.7	10.6	14.3	(x)	(x)	(x)
1 own child.............	18.7	17.4	26.1	16.6	15.8	23.5	(x)	(x)	(x)
2 own children..........	28.6	29.9	22.2	26.0	26.4	24.9	(x)	(x)	(x)
3 or more own children ..	40.6	41.8	37.7	45.7	47.3	37.3	(x)	(x)	(x)
Size of Family									
2 persons	11.1	7.7	25.9	10.3	7.7	24.8	(x)	(x)	(x)
3 persons	15.9	14.2	24.0	14.2	13.0	24.5	(x)	(x)	(x)
4 persons	27.2	28.9	19.2	24.7	25.5	19.9	(x)	(x)	(x)
5 persons	22.6	24.7	13.0	22.5	23.8	13.5	(x)	(x)	(x)
6 persons	12.0	12.7	9.1	14.5	15.4	8.2	(x)	(x)	(x)
7 or more persons.......	11.2	11.8	8.9	13.9	14.6	9.0	(x)	(x)	(x)

X Not applicable.

¹Includes families with a male head, but no spouse present, not shown separately.

Source: U.S. Bureau of the Census, *Current Population Reports*, Series P-20, No. 291, "Household and Family Characteristics: March 1975." Washington, D.C.: U.S. Government Printing Office, 1976.

ing their claws and theories as to its ultimate effect on children. Split custody is becoming more prevalent, with the same-sex parent having a better chance in court-awarded custody.

Even among visitation fathers, there is an effort to make the children feel more like an integral part of the fathers' lives and households than like a drop-in visitor.

The *New York Times Magazine* of February 1, 1976, featured in its interior design section specially designed space for children who spent weekends with their fathers. Needless to say, the budget for such custom-made innovations was not within the realm of most middle-class fathers. The article, heavily illustrated, was entitled "Life With (Divorced) Father," and provoked the following letter to the editor:

> Certainly the object of the three projects was to provide the child with a sense of "concern" and "belonging." Does the expenditure of two, three or five thousand dollars to create a gimmick which . . . integrates the child into the father's life for forty-eight hours achieve this end? . . . The questions which Miss Castan [the author] does not pose are why the father evidences a need to display his concern for the child . . . and whether providing . . . an elaborate jungle gym . . . communicates loving and caring?
>
> Michael Markowitz
> Brooklyn, N.Y.[1]

We do not know whether or not Mr. Markowitz is a weekend father. If he is a divorced father like many of those we have spoken to, who have to take care of their children's overnight arrangements with sleeping bags, we can well understand his resentment at the implication that an expenditure of several thousand dollars is synonymous with loving and caring.

There are fathers whose visitation privileges are based on "the letter of the law." These are the fathers who pick up their children every Sunday at 11:00 A.M. and return them promptly at 6:00 P.M. Some of them can maintain open telephone communication with their children, others cannot. They are no longer content with a Bozo the Clown image, having to amuse, entertain, or distract their

---

1. "Letters to the Editor," *New York Times,* 22 February, 1976.

children to fill up the time. They want to interact meaningfully with their children.

Then there are the fathers who envy the Bozo the Clown fathers who, at least, they say, get a chance to see their children. These men are fighting a bang-your-head-against-the-wall battle simply in an attempt to get court-ruled visitation rights enforced. Many of them are fighting to be able to reach their children by telephone, or even mail.

In order to understand the trend of fathers fighting for their rights as participating parents, custodial or otherwise, we will have to take a closer look at changing social mores over the past ten years, the women's movement, the sexual revolution, and their combined effect on the divorce rate, which far surpasses the 1-in-2.5 mark in many areas. It is not the number of divorces that is making the difference; it is the fact that divorce is making inroads among socioeconomic and cultural groups formerly considered, if not divorce-immune, at least low-risk.

"Divorce is becoming increasingly common among physicians," said Dr. Edward Stainbrook, a psychiatrist and chairman of the Department of Human Behavior at the University of California Medical School. He went on to say:

> A generation ago, the divorced doctor was the exception, now he is almost the rule. While no one, including the Census Bureau and medical societies, has collected statistics pointing toward a high divorce rate among doctors, physicians interviewed agreed that such was the case. One doctor here said that every doctor in his department at a major hospital here [Los Angeles] was either divorced or in the process of getting divorced.[2]

Although focusing on doctors, the *Times* article does point up the increased divorce rate among formerly "stable" socioeconomic groups, i.e., where the two-parent home was considered the only suitable environment for raising children. The trend of fathers being willing to assume full responsibility of their children has also been commented on. Michael McFadden, author of *Bachelor Fatherhood*, was quoted as follows:

> There are no real statistics available, but the number of men who are willing to take total care of their children is increasing

2. "For Doctors' Wives, Clouds, But No Silver Linings," *New York Times*, 27 October, 1976.

rapidly. So is the number of women who are willing to give them up.

In interviewing some fifty of these men, I found they had one thing in common; most were very happy with their way of life, and the longer they were at the job of single parent, the better they liked it.[3]

At one point, "the best interests of the child" invariably meant mother custody. Even this theory is undergoing a slow—admittedly very slow—change.

Decisions like these [custody awarded to someone other than the biological mother] reflect not only an erosion of the traditional presumption in favor of mothers in custody disputes involving young children, but also an effort by courts—acting in response to societal change and new theories of parenthood—to decide, with more flexibility and sophistication than in the past, precisely what the "best interests" of a child are.[4]

McFadden, describing the custodial fathers in his sampling, was describing full-cooperation father-custody situations, where the father wanted full custody of the children and the mother wanted him to have it. Probably the best example of full cooperation in father custody that we encountered was in the home of Steve and his sons. The three older boys, Bucky, fourteen, and the ten-year-old twins, Russ and Rick, stayed with Steve in his rambling, ten-room house in a suburb of Manchester, Vermont, while four-year-old Ivan went to Arizona with his mother. At the time of the separation, Steve and his wife, Lorraine, both agreed that Ivan, then three, was strongly attached to her. They both feel that Ivan will probably want to live with Steve and the boys when he gets older and have told him that he can go back to Steve whenever he wants. Steve was apprehensive when Lorraine and Ivan left, but there is open telephone communication, and Steve feels that Ivan has a warm, open relationship with him and his brothers.

Steve feels that both he and Lorraine have benefited from the divorce and that the improvement in their lives is bound to have a

3. Jean Perry, "Mom Goes Off to Find Herself: Dad Minds the Kids," *New York Daily News*, 1 April, 1975.

4. Lawrence Van Gelder, "New Custody Customs: In the 'Best Interests' of the Child," *New York Times*, 30 October, 1976.

favorable effect on the children. When we were in Steve's home, our interview was often interrupted by children, cats, and dogs, all coming to see the boys, kids and animals alike stopping for a quick hug with Steve.

Not every custodial father we spoke to had a situation running as smoothly as Steve's. In fact, a large percentage of custodial fathers have the children "by default"—their wives simply "wanted out," while they, themselves, had considered the marriage stable and their family life satisfactory. This situation is described most poignantly in Albert Martin's book, *One Man, Hurt.* In this book, Martin describes the anguish and emotional turmoil he underwent as he tried to understand his wife's anger, resentment, and hostility and expresses his futile efforts to maintain the marriage. He goes on to describe the bleakness in his own life and the lives of his three sons as a result of the divorce. He is not one of McFadden's typical happy-go-lucky custodial fathers.

Most custody battles do not begin until after the divorce. Elliott, who obtained custody of his two daughters after a fifteen-month court battle, told us frankly that he was terrified at the idea of taking custody, but when the effects of Gloria's drinking problem could no longer be ignored, he realized he would have to fight.

Nathan considers his custody a windfall. Divorced for six years, he has had custody of his two sons, seventeen and fifteen, and his daughter, eleven, for the last three. Nathan wanted custody from the beginning, but his lawyer told him, "Stop being a fool; be grateful for what you've got." He considered himself fortunate that his visitation was open and flexible, the children stayed with him weekends, and he had open visitation and telephone communication during the week.

Nathan's stroke of luck came about with Irene's announcement of her forthcoming marriage. The new husband wasn't exactly overjoyed about inheriting a ready-made family, and the kids wanted to live with Nathan anyway.

Ken, whom we met at the breakfast table in chapter 1, is biding his time about his six-year-old son, Brian, although Ellen, his daughter, constantly insists that he "do something." Actually Ken has legal custody of Brian, who stayed with him when his wife, Florence, left. One day Florence presented herself to the baby-sitter and said she was taking Brian "for a ride." The ride was 325 miles long, and its destination was Florence's apartment in New York, where Brian has remained ever since.

Ken is in no hurry either to "snatch" Brian or to take the battle to court, although he does have legal custody. Florence has worked herself up to a $30,000-a-year job, and Ken feels that Brian will become a nuisance to her in a short time.

"Besides," Ken states confidently. "*I* am the primary parent and I always was. Florence can compete with me and outdo me in the workaholic department and I'm not about to upstage her. But she can't touch me when it comes to children, either ours or anyone else's. She knows it now and she's always known it. It's just a matter of time before Brian subtly lets her know that she is a complete washout as a parent."

Murray is not as nonchalant as either Nathan or Ken. He cannot wait for a stroke of luck or his wife's indifference. Scott, his five-year-old son, is showing signs of serious disturbance. He describes the divorce: "Sure, like so many other couples we were having problems. One Friday she came and took the silver and all her belongings. The next day she came back and took Scott. She said she wanted to 'do her own thing' and open a boutique. So I gave her the money for it. All I cared about was that Scott would get proper care and we could explain it to him, not have him snatched from his home and his father just like that."

Scott is a shy youngster who cries easily and clings to Murray whenever someone approaches. He is in a therapy program for young children, but Murray sometimes wonders aloud, "Am I trying to bail out the Titanic with a thimble?"

"She's an attractive woman," Murray says, speaking of Sharon, his former wife. "Of course I expected her to have boyfriends."

He waits until Scott is out of earshot: "But does it have to be a different guy every night, and with Scott in the same room?"

Murray shakes his head. "I got a temporary order for custody. Who knows when he'll be taken away from me? My lawyer says he thinks we've got a chance, you know, with her having so many guys. But what am I going to do? Have some social worker question Scott as to what his mommy has been doing in bed?"

Murray asks us if we know of some program where men can learn things like cooking for kids.

"Sure, I can broil a steak," he tells us. "But it gets expensive. I can cook other things too, but kids don't go for the same food that we do. I can't go on with peanut butter and jelly sandwiches forever."

Whatever the estimates are of divorced fathers having custody, and guesses usually range from 5 to 15 percent, Tony Gil of the Family Law Counsel of New Jersey feels that it does not accurately reflect the percentage of *court-awarded* custody to fathers, which he feels is closer to 2 percent.

The problem of the father desiring custody is how much damage the child will suffer as a result of the court battle. Under the present adversary system, where the parent desiring custody has to prove the "unfitness" of the other parent, the one who will stoop the lowest in mudslinging, slander, character defamation, perjury, and vilification of the other is the one who has the best chance of gaining custody or, in the eyes of the law, being declared the most "fit" parent.

The concept of a father asking for custody of young children is one that provokes reactions of fear, amusement, puzzlement, anger, not to mention the "maternal instinct" response from both men and women. It is the women, however, who are threatened on a gut level. Following are some of the reactions we got:

"Men simply can't cope," said a married mother of two.

"Men don't want custody because it would interfere with their dating," declared a thirty-two-year-old divorcée.

"It would be too humiliating for the mother," from a suburban mother of two teen-agers.

A child psychologist, lecturing at a single-parents' meeting told us she "seriously doubts that a father can give the kind of love a mother can. After all, the mother had the child for nine months *in utero.*" Win did not get a chance to ask her what would happen if the mother had a miserable pregnancy; Ira wanted to ask her how long the father had the child in sperm.

"Are you trying to take *everything* away from the wife in a divorce?" asked one irate mother.

"No man wants or is able to care for children. They're just trying to get out of support payments," said a politically active feminist.

"Charlie would fall apart completely if he ever had to change a diaper," the mother of a five-month-old infant assured us.

The question that came to our minds was, "Just how did these men who had custody manage their children?" or, "If they were trying for custody, how did they think they would be able to manage?"

When Jerry, who recently gained custody of his seven-year-old daughter and five-year-old son, was asked, "What do you know about supermarket specials, best times for white sales, shopping for children, cooking and cleaning, and how to sort the wash for the machine?" the answer came back promptly: "The same thing you do."

Most of the men (and many women, incidentally) who can afford it have household help, at least part of the time. But more significant is the fact that the women's movement has affected the concept of traditional family roles. While role reversal may have been an initial goal of the women's movement as they deplored role-playing, for our purposes it would be more accurate to speak of role-deadlocking. The question is not so much whether the women's movement broke the deadlock of husband as wage earner only, never lifting a finger in household tasks, as it is how accurate that stereotype was long before the advent of the women's movement.

Granted, men may never have been enthusiastic about slipping into ruffled aprons, but does that mean they were either the domineering chauvinist pigs or the Harry Helpless the feminist movement and the women's service magazines led us to believe they were? Even if they balked at helping with household chores during marriage, how many men have never fried an egg, washed a dish, or bathed the baby?

Many of the full-custodial fathers we spoke to calmly answered that they had "taken over" rather than "helped out with" full household chores prior to the divorce. Others answered that the adjustment was quite difficult, but they had gotten over the hump somehow.

"You learn," Jerry told us, tersely.

"It's a question of organization. Same as a new project on the job," Phil, an electrical engineer, told us.

Whatever the actual figure of full-custodial fathers may be, Tony Gil believes, "For every father who has custody, fifteen visitation fathers are fighting for it."

With the current spotlight on male–female roles and rising cries for equality on the part of women, new stereotypes are emerging as a result of raised consciousnesses. The new mythology depicting many men as chauvinist pigs says something about the father role as well. By feminist definition, the male chauvinist pig is incapable either of emotion or of displaying emotion, more oriented toward technology than human feeling, regards all housework and child-care chores as "shitwork," and will not be bothered with it.

Where child-raising is concerned, he is not only completely indifferent to his child's well-being but, in addition, holds the status of "distinguished guest" in his child's eyes as contrasted to the "drudge" status of the mother. He will reluctantly, if at all, occasionally give the child a bath or baby-sit resentfully while the mother is out. His self-image is purported to undergo havoc if his wife tentatively suggests the idea of a career of her own, necessitating shared roles in housework and child care.

If so many men not only are completely indifferent to children emotionally, but see as their only goals in marriage total evolution of themselves while their wives wither away, why, then, are they fighting for custody, which would mean trading in the fabled "swinging bachelor life" not only for child care plus a career, but for the dreaded household tasks in addition? Is it strictly to avoid alimony and child-support payments? The financial argument could have held water thirty or forty years ago when divorce was most prevalent in upper-income and/or celebrity circles. In that milieu, a custodial mother could demand, in addition to a settlement reaching $1,000,000 or more for herself, considerably more in order to maintain the child in the barest of necessities—private schools, town houses with required nursemaids and servants, vacation homes, chauffeurs, and, of course, a suitable wardrobe for mother. In this set, child care meant devising the most fashionable way to get rid of children via nurses, maids, governesses, boarding schools, and camps. A father fighting for custody in those days could be said, with some accuracy, to be fighting for custody of his money.

The father of today is fighting for custody of his children for different reasons. The primary reason is that many women no longer feel the sense of responsibility in child-raising that they once did. No one can deny the degree to which the women's movement has downgraded the role of child-raising, especially if the mother has been educated above the high school level. Maureen Green, in her book, *Fathering*, states:

> Many feminists do not really think that women should be mothers at all. Rather than cope with redesigning or reinvolving father, they are tempted to abolish children. One of the most brilliant American leaders, Shulamith Firestone, while diagnosing that women's problems are centered in the fact that they are "neither insulated and protected from the larger world, as before, nor equipped to deal with it," rightly finds that "the heart of women's oppression is in her child-bearing and child-rearing roles." Her answer is basically that there shall be no more birth. It should all be handed over to the laboratory.[5]

5. Maureen Green, *Fathering* (New York: McGraw-Hill, 1976), p. 35.

Not all feminists are that extreme. But the unmistakable message from the women's movement is that the housewife/mother role is degrading to women, a complete turnabout from the famed (or notorious) "feminine mystique," which not only glorified child-raising but defined it as the only goal toward which women should aspire.

What about the women who have switched consciousness in midstream? What about the women who bore children during their *feminine* orientation only to regard them with sneering contempt during their *feminist* orientation? What about their children?

That is the question more and more fathers are asking. And it is why more and more fathers are fighting for custody.

4

ATTITUDES AND PLATITUDES

"Are you crazy?" Charlie looks incredulously at Ira. "That's twenty years ago you're talking about. What man would dare think about that twenty years ago?"

A group of us were sitting around Charlie's eclectic loft, supposedly to celebrate completion of the manuscript of Charlie's new book. As it turned out, the celebration was for Charlie's having received an extension on his deadline. Ira had just asked Charlie if he had tried to gain custody of his daughter.

"Twenty years ago no man would dare hope for custody," Charlie declared emphatically.

"The best we could hope for then," said Arnold, a soft-spoken man in his early fifties, "was that the day would come when our children might regard us as human beings and not the ogres we were made out to be."

"How does your daughter regard you today?" asks Jack, a visitation father trying to escape the Bozo the Clown snydrome.

Arnold is silent for a moment, then answers, looking off into space: "Emily and her husband are polite enough to me, but they made it quite clear that I'm better off not wearing out my twice-a-year welcome."

"And your grandson?" asks Charlie.

Arnold takes a deep breath before looking pensively into his wineglass. "He calls me 'my other Grandpa—the one who used to be Mommy's Daddy.' "

"What about me, Arnold?" asks Roger.

Roger, refused visitation despite court orders for the past year and a half, has just decided to fight *pro se* for custody. "Do I dare hope?"

"Get off your knees, Roger!"

Stan's voice has the ring of command to it. He leads a divorced fathers' group whose motto is "Self-defeat leads to legal defeat."

The rights of the divorced father is the other side of the equal rights coin and the side that the women's movement has chosen to overlook. The fact of the matter is that cultural, societal, and legal prejudices against a father obtaining custody or even having a say in the children's upbringing are far greater than the prejudices against women achieving economic equality in upper economic brackets. Legally, a man has about as much chance of getting "justice" in a custody or visitation case as a woman has in a rape case. In either situation, the odds are pitifully low.

June and William Noble, whose book, *The Custody Trap* is regarded as one of the most comprehensive works on the subject, state: "Custody means control. It means ownership, power, authority. In our highly competitive system there is nothing better than having control of something. In the end there's the custody award—the prize both parents seek."[1]

A prize which, as Tony Gil would say, men can hope for exactly 2 percent of the time. For many fathers, the battle for custody is the only route they can consider if they hope to cling to the merest thread of a relationship with their children.

The media are only beginning to spotlight the role of the father in the custody question. The subject has received very little attention prior to 1975. An article in the Chicago *Suburban Tribune* in August 1976 presents the following attitudes:

> "Never represent the man"—a law school professor to students in a divorce law course.
>
> "We want to live with Daddy"—children to a circuit court judge.
>
> "She'd have to be a drunk, a drug addict, or a prostitute before you should really fight for custody"—attorney to his male client.
>
> "Men who want and aren't getting custody are locked into

1. June and William Noble, *The Custody Trap* (New York: Hawthorn Books, 1975), p. 69.

roles.... Even lawyers discourage men from challenging custody."[2]

As far back as June 1973, radio station WLS in Chicago broadcasted an editorial that stated in part:

> WLS agrees with those who say current divorce provisions are a clear violation of men's constitutional rights. Imposed upon in the past, it is now time for the husband to be given more equitable treatment. ... The American divorce situation is the subject of many jokes and cartoons. It isn't funny to men.[3]

An article in the *Boston Sunday Herald* in July 1976 includes the following:

> In Massachusetts, some lawyers, legislators, judges, parents and psychologists complain that the probate system discriminates against men in divorce and custody cases and deprives them of their rights as parents. Traditionally, the court has inferred that after a divorce, a man's responsibility for his children is strictly financial. The emotional, psychological and moral obligations of the male parent to his children are often overlooked.[4]

The same article touched upon the most emotionally loaded aspect of the divorced father's dilemma—that of his total legal vulnerability if he should default on support (and sometimes alimony) payments, coupled with his legal impotence in getting visitation rights enforced. Quoting Judge Haskell Freedman of Middlesex Probate Court: "Another mother looked me right in the eye and said she wouldn't let her ex-husband near the children. Sure she was in contempt, but could I put the mother of three in jail?"[5]

Judge Freedman was asked by a member of a Fathers United group

2. Cissi Falligant, "If Marriage Ends Up in Court, ADAM's There for Advice," Chicago *Suburban Tribune,* 4 August, 1976.

3. Radio editorial, WLS (Chicago), ABC affiliate, broadcasted various times June 15–18, 1973.

4. Laura White, "New Pattern Emerges for Children of Divorce," *Boston Sunday Herald Advertiser,* 18 July, 1976, Section 6, p. A-11.

5. Ibid.

in Boston if it weren't true that the father would be jailed promptly if he reneged on his financial obligations:

"Yes," says Judge Freedman. "That would happen."[6]

Daniel Molinoff is a lawyer who has questioned legal precedent and tradition. He has two overwhelming reasons for doing so—his sons, Michael, seven, and Joel, five. When Molinoff speaks of the situation, it is difficult to fathom whether he is speaking primarily as a lawyer or as a father:

> You may think that your children "belong" to you as well as to your wife. According to contemporary judicial practices and prejudices, they do not. They are hers. If you or your wife decide to end the marriage, most likely the courts, automatically and arbitrarily, will give her their custody. In this day of ever-increasing equal rights for women, minority groups and the poor, fathers in this state, as far as custody of children is concerned, are essentially without rights.[7]

Molinoff refers to New York when he writes of "this state," but fathers in the other forty-nine feel he is speaking for them as he continues:

> Section 70 of the Domestic Relations Law states in part that there shall be "no prima facie right to the custody of the child in either parent," but traditionally our courts have ignored the spirit of the law. The presumption in New York is that, unless proven otherwise, the mother is more fit to be the custodial parent because she is the mother. The father is, therefore, deemed unfit because he is the father.
>
> The major reason for this discrimination is the basic conservatism of the two courts that have concurrent jurisdiction in these matters, the New York State Supreme and Family Courts. The judges, most of whom are men and fathers, bring to the bench the belief that children belong with their mothers. Traditionally, fathers earned money and mothers stayed at home to raise the children. If the marriage was dissolved, the children were usually awarded to the mother. Today, many

6. Ibid.
7. Daniel D. Molinoff, "Father Knows Best," *New York Times*, 24 June, 1975, p. 43.

mothers have both careers and children, but the notion that a mother must still be the custodial parent persists.[8]

Virtually every state has the equivalent of the "no prima facie right to the custody of the child in either parent" somewhere on the books. The reaction of any father fighting for custody, if confronted with that phrase, would be similar to the reaction of Gloria Steinem if someone were to tell her that women have equal rights in employment.

Representing Molinoff in his joint-custody case was Doris Sassower, who was also called in for consultation in the Cornell joint-custody case (see page 22). Sassower's credentials are impressive in legal as well as feminist circles. Organizations for which she has served include the Institute on Women's Wrongs, Association of Feminist Consultants, and she is a founder of the Professional Women's Caucus. Her published writings include "The Role of Lawyers in Women's Liberation," (*New York Law Journal*, December 30, 1970), "The Legal Profession and Women's Rights," (*Rutgers Law Review*, Fall 1970) and "Women, Power and the Law" (*ABA Journal*, May 1976). Sassower may be one of the few feminists who is not afraid to speak up in areas involving *human* equality. "Feminism," said attorney Sassower,

> should convey the concept of shared responsibility and freedom from stereotypes. In general, feminists have not been sufficiently liberated to leave the care of their children to their father.
>
> As more and more women go out in the world and become emancipated, become involved in a career and a job, I think they will appreciate a father who wants to relieve them of the worries of who is going to take care of the children while they are on the job.[9]

The article, which spotlighted the Molinoff case, spotlights the passive attitude of many divorcing fathers:

> Mr. Molinoff says that he has many friends whose wives have said that they did not want to be married any more. "So the

8. Ibid.

9. Jo Ann Levine, "Parents Agree to Joint Custody," *Christian Science Monitor*, 5 May, 1975, p. 7.

husbands walked calmly to the showers, packed their bags, took their TV and favorite painting and their car, and left the wife, the house and the insurance policy, thinking, 'That's the way it should be. Society has determined that women should be custodians of my children, so if they say go, I go.'

"I did the same thing. I walked out. I walked out carrying my suitcase full of clothes, my law books, and I suddenly brought myself up short and said, 'What am I doing? I'm doing what everybody else has done.' And I decided not to walk away."[10]

The following interchange took place during a convention of the American Bar Association in May 1976, in Atlanta, between Doris Sassower and other members of the Family Law Section:

At this point Doris Sassower of New York City asked about techniques advisable when representing the father in a custody dispute where the mother is not unfit. I would definitely tell that father not to try, and I think that to represent a man in such a case "is unethical and any attorney who would do it should be disbarred," said Stanton L. Ehrlich of Chicago. Julia Perles was in full agreement: to promote a custody fight by agreeing to represent a man where the wife is not an unfit parent is unethical, she said. At this point the questioner and many members of the audience insisted loudly that the panelists must have misunderstood the question. They were not recognized, but Ehrlich said that he had understood the question perfectly well: should you represent a man in a custody contest where the mother is not unfit, so that obviously the man is litigating solely out of vindictiveness? Perles seconded this. Sassower said that the panelists' intuitive "perfect understanding" of the question said more about ingrained prejudices among lawyers and judges in the domestic relations field than any poll or survey could hope to do.[11]

This was not the first occasion on which Doris Sassower incurred the wrath of her legal colleagues. The following excerpt is from the ABA convention of the previous year, when she first brought up the question of equal consideration for fathers in custody disputes. She

10. Ibid.
11. Family Law Reporter, 2 FLR 2688, 7 August, 1976.

had just won joint custody in the Molinoff case over determined opposition by the mother.

> Ms. Sassower stressed that what many fathers now want is not just extended visitation, but true parental rights: i.e., an equal voice in decisions affecting the child's future. She was immediately attacked by numerous male members of the panel and the audience, who unequivocally declared that (1) any father who says he wants extended visitation or continued parental rights is a liar, who is merely seeking to harass the wife in order to pry into her new social life and exert pressure that will force down her monetary demands, and (2) that any attorney who argues such a position is irresponsibly focusing on the parents' opposing rights and ignoring the best interest of the child's since everyone knows that shuttling back and forth is bad for a child's well-being, and (3) that anyone who obtains an order for joint custody has merely proved that the judge was too soft hearted and opposing counsel was untalented. *It was again roundly asserted that paternal love is a myth* [italics ours]. . . . Sassower was not allowed to defend her viewpoint, for the program had to be moved along, but she told FLR[12] that such arguments show how ingrained the sex prejudice of earlier generations' assumptions are. The judge in her case . . . said most of these same things. He was convinced that the father must be lying, and at first he simply could not imagine a father really wanting to care for a child at home rather than working five days a week.[13] [14]

As to the argument presented that shuttling the children between two homes would be too traumatic:

> . . . she [Sassower] also queried whether a single parent having sole custody does not subject the child to just as much shuttling and uncertainty as retention of the father as joint custodian would mean. Between working and dating the wife is likely to leave the child with sitters about half the time, and the in-

12. *Family Law Reporter*, 1 FLR 2708, 26 August, 1975.

13. Molinoff has since arranged his work schedule to allow him more time with the children.

14. *Family Law Reporter*, 1 FLR 2708, 26 August, 1975.

terested father may protest that he should not have to pay for her babysitters when he is perfectly willing to do the "babysitting" himself.[15]

The same panel spotlights the legal point of view on other aspects of custody:

A reform repeatedly suggested throughout the sessions was bifurcation of proceedings so that custody is decided after the divorce is final and the husband and wife, secure in their liberation from each other, are more at ease. *However, it was generally agreed that the cleverest lawyers refuse to let their clients agree to bifurcation, for the simple reason that the longer one separated parent has sole custody of the children the more likely it is that the children will be insidiously convinced that they hate the absent parent* [italics ours]. The tragic thing, said John Conery, QC of Montreal, is that most children really do like both parents and it is not until after the separation that one parent's effective partisan brainwashing starts. He told an anecdote from his own practice, which pointly illustrated how fully children can conceal their love for the absent parent in order to please the custodial parent and her attorney—until the point where they are examined privily by the judge.

Another speaker voiced his opinion that more and more custody modifications are happening informally, when the child is dissatisfied with the custodial parent he—or more frequently, she—simply runs away, generally to show up at the noncustodial parent's door.[16]

Children showing up at the noncustodial parent's door does not necessarily guarantee an "informal custody modification," as Howard Pierson found out: "He spent seven years of his life fighting . . . before he was finally able to gain custody of his two young children."[17]

When Pierson's children, ages seven and eight, "simply showed up at his doorstep," he finally decided that he could not send them back. According to the account the Nobles give us in *The Custody Trap,*

15. Ibid.
16. Ibid.
17. Noble, *The Custody Trap,* p. 47.

"The children were overjoyed at his decision."[18] This joy was not shared by Pierson's ex-wife, who took him to court. The judge ordered the children returned to their mother. "It was a stiff blow to Howard and the children, but reluctantly they agreed to follow the judge's decision."[19]

The scene was reenacted with the children running away to their father, his ex-wife's demand that he return them, the same courtroom and the same judge: "Not only did he [Judge Halstead of Baltimore County Court] direct the children to go back with their mother, but he threatened that if they ran away again he would send them to an institution.[20]

Children's rights, anyone?

It is not only the traditional court prejudice against fathers gaining custody that the custodial father has to battle. The prejudice that "children always belong with their mother" has implications outside of the courtroom as well.

Molinoff describes some of the nonlegal problems he has had to face since he entered his joint-custody agreement.

"At first I was looked at as some kind of freak," he recalls. Most of the animosity, he feels, has come from women—mothers, teachers, and neighbors who felt he was joking or being vindictive toward his former wife at the children's expense. Many mothers who picked up their children from school wouldn't talk to him at first. One teacher was hostile and haughty.

Molinoff admits that he's now over the hump, and as far as societal attitudes are concerned, he has made progress.

"At first I was that dirty bastard who took the children away from their mother. Now I'm that individual who has joint custody."

Stuart never gained the acceptance that Molinoff did. Stuart has had custody of Jonathan, now six, since he was eighteen months old. The cooperative day nursery Jonathan attended was staffed by radical feminists. Each morning, when he dropped Jonathan off at the nursery, he was greeted with a chorus of "If there were equal rights, women wouldn't have to take care of children." Stuart never got very far when he tried to explain to them that he had full custody because his wife had left to join a hippie commune.

Bill, who has just started to fight *pro se* for custody of his seven-

18. Ibid., p. 48.
19. Ibid.
20. Ibid., p. 49.

year-old daughter, feels that the battle is tougher than any legal proceedings or Mrs. Grundy-type tongue-clicking.

"It's primarily a battle with yourself," explains Bill. "We've been brainwashed so much that we really have to ask ourselves if we're doing the best thing for our kids. Those psychologists tell us we're laying some kind of trip on ourselves, we're really not fit to bring up kids, you know, tiptoe out the door, don't rock the boat. Then they tell us we're damaging the kids, you know, the kid's going to be a pariah in the neighrobhood because she's living with her father. They keep asking us what we're trying to prove, why we're trying to compete with our wives, what's wrong with us that we can't accept the traditional masculine role, and are we having problems with our masculinity. We're supposed to be 'mature' about this whole thing— you know, keep the money rolling in, take the kid to the zoo on Sundays, but to show that you really care, don't forget to send a birthday card."

"Knock it off, Bill," warns Steve. "Get off your knees."

There's an ominous ring to Steve's voice. Charlie rushes in to smooth things over, the gallon bottle of wine poised over Bill's glass.

"Come on, come on, everybody," he announces, placatingly. "We'll all have some more wine. Give me your glass, Bill."

Roger shakes his head despairingly.

"Charlie dispenses that stuff like it was chicken soup."

Gently, Ira removes the bottle from Charlie's hands. "Knock it off, Charlie. Bill's had enough."

Bill has *obviously* had enough.

Deftly, Ira attempts to remove the glass from Bill's hand. "That's enough, Bill," he says. "Come on down to our meeting on Tuesday night."

Just as deftly, Bill holds on to his glass.

"Who the fuck do you think you are, Ira? Alcoholics Anonymous or something?"

"No," Ira shakes his head slowly. "I'm another father fighting for custody."

5

THE MATERNAL INSTINCT: MADONNAS, MEDEAS, MYTHS, AND MOVEMENTS

"Daddies Care" . . . "Dads Need Kids" . . . "Fathers Have Feelings Too" . . . "I Have a Paternal Instinct."

It was Father's Day, 1976. A march was organized in New York City's Washington Square and men, women, and children carried signs bearing the above slogans.

The demonstration was the brainchild of Warren Farrell, author of *The Liberated Man* and one of the more recognizable names in what is loosely known as the men's movement. Farrell (who is, incidentally, childless) decries male–female role-deadlocking, which creates, at best, half-persons. Involvement with children, he believes, reinforces rather than negates masculinity. He feels that the myth of the maternal instinct cheats both men and women:

> The motherhood myth is an amalgam of the following beliefs: every normal woman has a maternal instinct (but the father has no paternal instinct); a woman cannot be fulfilled without children; the mother's constant attention to *her* child is irreplaceable and beneficial; the father's attention is important in theory but "impractical" because of the demands of his role as breadwinner . . .; any woman who tries to deny these things is trying to be a man and should feel guilty about her lack of maternal love and the neglect of her children.[1]

1. Warren Farrell, *The Liberated Man: Beyond Masculinity: Freeing Men and Their Relationships with Women* (New York: Random House, 1976), p. 112.

Farrell is not the first person to attack the myth of motherhood and the maternal instinct. Rightly, it could be said that the women's movement is a backlash against the myth of the maternal instinct. But it is a powerful myth whose roots go back to antiquity. It is a dangerous myth because it presupposes that the biological act of giving birth automatically guarantees a lifelong mother–child bond that is unquestionably beneficial to both. It is dangerous because it leads to planned pregnancies and unwanted children. The automatic fitness of the biological mother presumption reaches its cruelest proportions when a child is snatched from adoptive parents who have proven their parental ability and returned to a mother whose parental ability is never even brought into question. It is a myth that is conveniently resurrected and dusted off periodically to suit the needs of various economic and political climates. It is a dangerous myth because the maternal instinct does not always coexist with and often preempts the parental consciousness.

One of the most insidious by-products of the myth of the maternal instinct is that as the mother is portrayed as the be-all and end-all in a child's life, the role of the father is negated in direct proportion.

The madonna and child scene is one of the most consistently recurring themes in Western art, equaled only by the Crucifixion, both of which reached their apex during the Renaissance. The expression *good woman* was synonymous with motherhood. Not only was the act of childbirth expected to weld the halo onto any woman, the omission of this incident in any woman's life relegated her to a position of pitied mediocrity at best and unnatural monsterhood at worst. Motherhood became the snake oil for all the ills of womanhood, having both preventive and curative powers. Not only was it alleged to confer the indelible stamp of "femininity" on any woman, it was also hailed as the cure for everything from restlessness to insanity. Indeed, the absence of this exalted state was regarded as an accurate diagnosis for any shortcoming in the character of any woman.

History books define the birth of Marie Antoinette's children as the turning point in her life from frenzied promiscuity to blissful serenity. In Greek mythology, the legendary jealousy of Hera, wife of Zeus, was attributed to her barren state. Mortal and goddess alike were known to quake when her wrath was aroused. Her inability to bear children was cited as the reason for Zeus's philandering on and off Mount Olympus, and the great god himself would assume many forms in order to achieve his end.

But it was Niobe, a mortal woman, who brought about the wrath of the gods by using her supermotherhood as claim for peerage with the gods. Her fourteen children, seven sons and seven daughters, were her pride. She was not about to partake in rites of worship for the goddess Latona, who had only two children:

> Have I not cause for pride? Will you prefer to me this Latona, the Titan's daughter, with her two children? I have seven times as many. . . . I feel myself too strong for Fortune to subdue. . . . Were I to lose some of my children, I should hardly be left as poor as Latona with her two only. Away with you from these solemnities . . . have done with this worship.[2]

When Latona began to doubt whether she was, indeed, a goddess, the wrath of the gods fell swiftly. Close upon that wrath came a shower of arrows, all directed at Niobe's children. When only one was left alive, Niobe

> . . . clasped [her] in her arms, and covered as it were with her whole body. "Spare me one, and that the youngest! O, spare me one of so many!" she cried; and while she spoke, that one fell dead.[3]

King Lear, upon learning of his daughter Goneril's treachery, curses her as follows:

> Hear, Nature, hear! dear goddess, hear!
> Suspend thy purpose, if thou didst intend
> To make this creature fruitful!
> Into her womb convey sterility!
> Dry up in her the organs of increase,
> And from her derogate body never spring
> A babe to honour her![4]

The theme keeps recurring: Saintliness and true womanhood are equated with motherhood; ruthlessness and cruelty are equated with nonmotherhood.

Like the proverbial 'eternal love that could not survive the hostile

---

2. Thomas Bullfinch, *Age of Fable or Beauties of Mythology* (Philadelphia: M. M. McKay, 1898), pp. 136, 137.
3. Ibid.
4. Shakespeare, *King Lear*, act 1, scene 4.

climate of marriage, so was the motherhood fantasy doomed to instant destruction with the intrusion of reality. The youth counter-culture of the 1960s created its own madonna myth in an attempt to counteract the "establishment" madonna myth: "Oh, it was beautiful to be the earth mother. It was middle America in the year 1966 . . . and many of us were pregnant . . . what else can you expect with free love . . . we were the Sweet Lorraines and Lady Madonnas and for nine months it was groovier than hell."[5]

But the nine-month dream ended: ". . . the summer of love came and with it the babies . . . babies in all their full bloom with wild cries that didn't fit earth mother and Lady Madonna images."[6]

What with Lady madonnas, earth mothers, and Sweet Lorraines, the motherhood mystique reached near-cult proportions in the United States following World War II until the onset of the women's movement, when it underwent a complete and rapid metamorphosis from salvation to damnation in a woman's self-development. As the mother–child tie tightened into near-strangulation for both, so did the father step out of the parenthood picture. His function, if it existed at all outside of impregnation, was to create an ideal canvas for the madonna image, preferably not adding any extraneous brush strokes of his own. The madonna image was further glorified when the Freudians picked up where the Fra Angelicos left off. Motherhood, circa the 1950s and early 1960s, guaranteed "emotional maturity" and "adjustment to life role," "acceptance of self," in addition to curing neurosis and penis envy, which were synonymous anyway. Male neurosis was simply castration fear, so they didn't have to be bothered with fatherhood. Instead of the manger, the mid-twentieth-century madonna held forth in split-level suburbia, and the mother who aspired toward the world beyond the lot on which her house was situated came to typify the ruthless woman of the 1950s and 1960s.

Sacrifices of mothers for their children are well-known throughout western literature. In fact, motherhood is synonymous with sacrifice. If the mother didn't sacrifice, she wasn't that much of a mother anyway or, even worse, lacked a maternal instinct.

Lesser known, and not quite as celebrated throughout Western civilization, are sacrifices on the part of mothers *of* their children. The

5. Margarita Donnelly, "Alternate-Culture Mirror America," *The Future of the Family*, ed. Louise Kapp Howe (New York: Simon & Schuster, 1972), p. 67.
6. Ibid.

expression "Hell hath no fury like a woman scorned" is best exemplified in Euripides' classic, *Medea,* whose heroine slays her children in order to obtain revenge against her unfaithful husband.

Tales of scorned women killing their children in order to punish unfaithful husbands have not appeared often since the advent of Christianity. Fortunately, mother love has been characterized more by mothers sacrificing *for* their children than sacrificing *of* their children. But who can blame so many divorced fathers for feeling that there may just be something of a Medea component in their custodial wives' treatment of the children the moment another woman enters the picture—often, months or years after the divorce has taken place?

> Former husbands, unless neurotically jealous, tend to go off in the woods to quietly lick their wounds. Former wives, particularly if they have no independent income and have not remarried, tend to use their talons. Some make a career out of that role.[7]

Describing a doctor who remarried while his wife did not:

> He gives her half his income and she still wants more. She dragged him into court so many times he was forced to move to the Midwest to escape her harassment. Occasionally he returns to Pennsylvania on business but comes clandestinely because there's always a judgment dangling over his head. On such visits he can't even see his kids for fear she'll blow the whistle.[8]

Another remarried father describes his situation as

> It's tough . . . because my first wife hates me and never lets up telling the kids what an SOB I am and what a slut I married.[9]

Whatever Medea-like characteristics a custodial mother may have displayed toward her husband in his attempts to maintain some form of relationship with his children following a divorce, for the present she is regarded as a madonna in the courtroom because she is the

---

7. Carol Saline, "Who's for Seconds?" *Philadelphia,* Sept. 1976, pp. 187, 188.
8. Ibid., p. 188.
9. Ibid., pp. 188, 189.

biological mother. With present legal proceedings in favor of the mother receiving custody, the twentieth-century Medea can get her talons in pretty deeply, with the backing of an entire justice system. Those talons can dig into the children as well as the father while, in the eyes of the law, her halo shines all the brighter.

The cult of motherhood came under attack most vociferously in the early days of the women's movement. At that time, leaders of divorced fathers' groups had hoped that a number of ideals voiced by the movement would combine to establish a divorced father as at least a participating parent and make some progress in establishing him as a fit custodial parent without having to prove the mother unfit. After all, equal responsibility for child care was one of the stated goals early in the feminist movement.

The concept of having fathers participate in child care satisfied different segments of the movement. To the feminists who believed that role-deadlocking was detrimental to both men and women, more father–child interaction would introduce a heretofore neglected area of fulfillment in the father's life. To the extremists, however, father–child interaction and a father's responsibility for the everyday care of his children would be a righteous punishment for him. Whatever the rationale, father's group leaders reasoned, the women's movement would stand behind them in bringing about some sort of equality to fathers in the parental role. Also, the movement's early statements to the effect that alimony was degrading to women offered a spark of light at the end of a pitch-black tunnel to lower- and middle-income men. That hope was scotched when the movement did one of its frequent flip-flops in the mid-seventies:

> If we lived in complete equality, and women earned as much as men, we wouldn't need to consider alimony. . . . I don't like the word "alimony" because it somehow connotes taking advantage of sex. Nor do we feminists like the terms "maintenance," which assumes the woman is like an automobile, or "allowance," which assumes she's a child. So we've developed the concept of entitlement.
>
> Entitlement is the equivalent of severance pay for work done at home during the length of the marriage and is a fee above and beyond child support.[10]

10. Betty Friedan, "Should You Accept Alimony?" *Harper's Bazaar*, July 1976, pp. 45, 87.

Betty Friedan goes on to explain the reversal in feminist thinking:

> In the early days of the Movement, we fell into a trap when we said, "No alimony!" because housewives who divorced were in terrible straits. We fell into another trap by accepting no-fault divorce without provision for mandatory economic settlement.[11]

No matter how shrill the cries were that men should shoulder their share of the responsibility of child care, the concept of men taking full custody of children has been met with cries of indignation and outrage on the part of the women's movement. The "spite" factor, they maintain, is the men's only motive.

In spite of the mystique of the maternal instinct which still prevails, more recent thought has come up with theories such as "the psychological parent" and "the primary parent." Psychologists assure us that except for rare mutations, this psychological and/or primary parent is inevitably the mother. The women's movement has been about as amenable to the concept that a father may want custody because he considers himself the primary parent as many industry leaders have been amenable to the concept that women want executive responsibility and remuneration for motives other than castration.

Constance Woodruff, chairperson of the New Jersey Advisory Commission of the Status of Women had the following to say about the seven fathers who brought a class action suit against the state of New Jersey in visitation-custody action: "The increase in fathers seeking custody of their children is part of a backlash against the women's liberation movement. Traditions are very deep-rooted. We all fall victim to our prejudices. These men are assuming they're not going to get a fair shake in court."[12]

Carlo Basile, one of the men involved in the action, who has been in court seventy-six times in the past twenty-eight months seeking visitation, might have an articulate answer to Ms. Woodruff, not all of it printable.

It is true that straws of change are in the wind. Dr. Doris Jonas Freed of New York, a matrimonial attorney, an author, and chairper-

11. Ibid., p. 87.
12. Jim Benson, "Men Make Claim to Equal Rights, Too," *Hudson* (N.J.) *Dispatch*, 18 Dec. 1976.

son of the divorce committee of the American Bar Association's Family Law Division, stated that "there is a 'great possibility' of discrimination against fathers in custody cases. But . . . there is a definite trend towards desexing custody as well as desexing child and job support."[13]

Quite a few men would like to see this trend accelerate. On the same Father's Day when Warren Farrell's group was demonstrating carrying signs that read, "Fathers Have Feelings, Too," the National Organization of Women was demonstrating in Connecticut with a slogan of its own: "Give Dad a Subpoena for Father's Day."

Maternal instinct, anyone?

13. Ibid.

6

THE FATHER IMAGE: THE LITTLE MAN WHO WASN'T THERE

Fatherhood meant delivering, or not delivering, checks. It meant being around, or being unwelcome when around. It meant either shouting, or that soul-crushing silence most deeply installed in the soul of any red-blooded American boy: Dad mute behind his newspaper. Dad losing an argument. Dad standing alone watering the lawn, wooden as a dead post—while inside the household lived that real life in which he didn't count. Fatherhood, and to that degree manhood, meant being feared, or ignored, or despised, or pitied, or hated.[1]

Thus, Stephen Koch describes fatherhood in the 1950s and 1960s, from a son's point of view. Koch's excellent, oft-quoted article is one of the few that deals with the subject of man and his fatherhood identity in the days when the madonna mystique reigned supreme. The father became the cipher parent when the feminine mystique characterized family life.

It was not always that way. From the awe and dignity of the Old Testament patriarch down to the high-collared Victorian paterfamilias, the very word *father* could conjure up awe, respect, and fear equal to that of an authoritarian clergyman. His manner ran the gamut from benevolence to despotism (sometimes combining the two), vascillating from harsh and condemning to kind and forgiving;

1. Stephen Koch, "The Guilty Sex: How American Men Became Irrelevant," *Esquire*, July 1975, pp. 53, 54.

his word, his expression, his very look could mean the difference between sunshine and gloom in the lives of his wife and children. He was never depicted as providing infants with physical care, either keeping them clean or feeding them. His role was more one of dispensing wisdom and blessings. This is best personified in Polonius's advice to his son, Laertes: "This above all, to thine own self be true."

But, from the bearded patriarch dispensing deep-baritone wisdom to the mustachioed paterfamilias bellowing indignation because someone had the temerity to sit in "his" chair during his absence, another image of fatherhood emerged, aided and abetted by "wholesome entertainment" via the family hour on television: The boob who paid the bills.

Maureen Green, in *Fathering*, sums up the situation in a chapter entitled "The Decline of Father."

> No one is taking any notice of father.
>
> As any suburban father will testify, today's family does not fall into a respectful hush when father starts to speak. But that's only part of it. Much more ruthlessly, father is being ignored by the experts. As a topic, as a subject for research and conjecture by sociologists, by revolutionaries and journalists, father is forgotten. They are all too busy concentrating on mother.
>
> However underprivileged women may still consider they are in many aspects of modern life, they are overindulged in terms of the number of words devoted to them. Fifty years ago, Virginia Woolf called woman "The most discussed animal in the universe." Women are still an obsessive topic, the center of all attention as they churn over their options, their rights and their duties. Millions of miles of newsprint have been devoted to just one aspect of women's lives—motherhood. By comparison, men get very little attention at all; and when they do, popular interest seems to center on men as aggressors, as hunters. Man as family man, as father, is rarely on the agenda.[2]

What effect has this cipherization of fatherhood had on fathers? Equally significant, what effect has it had on their children? Kenneth Howard describes the cipherization of his own father:

2. Maureen Green, *Fathering* (New York: McGraw-Hill, 1976), pp. 1, 2.

In later years, my mother waged a ceaseless struggle . . . designed—albeit unconsciously—to weld my brother, my mother and me into a tight and intimate squad capable of humiliating my father every time he entered the house, of making him look like an incompetent, a fool, an object of disdain.[3]

Howard goes on to describe the effect on his father:

My brother and I were encouraged to hurl abuse along with her. She taught us to pounce with sarcastic glee on every minor grammatical mistake Dad made as he attempted to defend himself. . . . By the time I was ten, my father had become so overwhelmed by these assaults that for a brief period (he recently admitted) he actually hated me, belittling me when I was alone with him as vehemently as I did him during those sessions at the dinner table.[4]

When the feminine mystique held sway, a woman could establish her womanhood in the mother role and the mother role only. Any interest of developing aspects of herself in addition to the mother role would have jeopardized her "maternal instinct" and, consequently, her womanhood status. Conversely, a man could establish his manhood in everything *except* the father role. Masculinity was personified by a combination of superior earning ability, excellence in sports, "love-'em-and-leave-'em" attitude toward women, and a total disdain of involvement with children, which could have left him open to a charge of "homosexuality," the epithet designed to do for a man's self-image what the charge of "no maternal instinct" would do for a woman's.

The women's media portrayed women in the mother role only. The only publication that recognizes men in the father role that we can think of is *Parent's* magazine, and we have no way of knowing how many men read it. Generally the male media break down into roughly three categories: (1) business and financial, characterized by the *Wall Street Journal*; (2) sports, as characterized by *True* and *Sports Illustrated*; and (3) sexual, reflected in the "skin" magazines—

3. Kenneth Howard, "An Overdose of Mother Love," *Cosmopolitan*, November 1976, p. 136.
4. Ibid., p. 138.

Playboy, Penthouse, etc. None of these publications has devoted much space to the father role as a basic component of manhood.

Exactly how did this come about? The answer is not an easy one to pin down and certainly one that was not seriously sought until recent years.

During the 1950s and 1960s, the father's role was limited to his earning capacity and emotional support of his wife in her mother role, preferably with no interference. After all, she was the one who read Dr. Spock and all the other books and magazines about child care. Dad's role was limited to occasional walk-ons in crucial periods of his children's lives, something like the following:

His role in impregnating the mother has always been acknowledged. After that, where the mass media were concerned, he chain-smoked nervously in the hospital waiting room until a kindly doctor reassured him with a slap on the back, "Don't worry, we've never lost a father yet, ha ha!" If the baby was a boy, Dad was depicted as immediately rushing right out to his nearest sporting goods store and buying an array of baseball equipment that could make any major league pitcher look underprivileged. If it was a girl, he promised to do better next time. Once the baby was home, his adeptness at physical handling of the infant could roughly be compared to the stereotype of a woman trying to change the spark plugs in a recalcitrant automobile. Knowledgeable Moms tittered as Dad hopelessly tried to figure out just which end of the baby it was that went into a diaper, and besides, the logistics of folding said diaper reputedly had the power to reduce a structural engineer to a mass of hopelessness and thumbs.

Until the time a grown child left home for reasons of college or marriage, he had several walk-on roles, all of them vague. One of the classics of the Father Soft Shoe repertory was supposed to have taken place when his son (never his daughter) asked him where babies came from. This was clearly the occasion for a "man-to-man" talk. As he stuttered over allusions to birds and bees, his seven-year-old son finally interrupted him with, "But, Dad, you forgot about the part where the father puts his penis into the mother's vagina."

From time to time, a few theories were developed as to how a father could participate more fully in the lives of his children. These included a sort of midwife-apprentice role if his wife had decided upon natural childbirth, which was supposed to give him a feeling of participation. A "pal" movement was afoot for awhile in the late 1950s, but it was short-lived. Various spurts of father activity—such as bathing the children—were recommended and endorsed by the women's service magazines but abandoned shortly thereafter. (Dad probably left a ring around the bathtub.)

In middle-class suburbia, a father's attending a PTA meeting could have earned him an award of merit certificate as an involved father. Most of Dad's interaction was supposed to have been limited to his son, admonishing him to "be a man" and encouraging him in principles of sportsmanship with shouts of "Kill 'em, son. That's right, kill 'em!" during Little League activity. If he were to acknowledge the existence of a daughter at all, it was to notice a new dress and to assure her that she was "Daddy's sweetheart."

As his children entered the teen years, Dad was expected to be reasonable and cooperative in handing over the keys to the family car on demand, at least until his son reached his sixteenth birthday, on which occasion he simply handed over an entire car. At that time, father–son interaction was best characterized by a "Drive safely, son, and don't forget to observe the speed limits."

His authority where his teen-aged daughter was concerned was usually limited to some flaccid attempts to cajole her into returning home from dates "at a reasonable hour," only to be answered by a tearful "But, Dad, *all* the kids can stay out and have a good time," or a lofty, superior "Oh, Dad, how can you be so square!"

Dad's participating role in his children's upbringing underwent a sudden spurt when his children were in college, mostly in check-writing activity. His *moment suprême*, however, arrived in anticipation of his daughter's wedding. His exasperation at the mounting bills was met with cries of "But Dad, a wedding is something every girl has always *dreamed* of" from his daughter, in concert with his wife's "But, darling, a girl only gets married *once*."

Lovable boob that he was, Dad had to be kept gently but firmly in his place. And his place in child-rearing was roughly comparable to Mom's place in the board room of General Motors—in other words, the farther away the better. Is it any wonder that he retreated behind the *Wall Street Journal*, *True*, *Playboy*, or to a chair in front of the television set?

The expression "mother knows best" was more applicable to the father who tried to have a say in his children's upbringing than it did to the children who suddenly decided they wanted to wear their sneakers out in a snowstorm.

In his parent role, father was the puppet whose strings were pulled by the "primary parent"—namely, the mother. Parenthood was her field of expertise, as moneymaking was or was supposed to be his. The father role was mainly that of husband of the mother, a role whose rules and regulations were carefully spelled out by the women's service magazines. To the best of our research efforts, the prime requisite in this role was to have a lean jaw.

The stereotype of Dad as bumbling fool was capitalized on by Madison Avenue. Evidently, the efficiency of a household product was understood to be beyond the pale when it was accompanied by the slogan, "Even a *husband* can do it." But those were the good old days, when a father's function was to play Mother's Little Helper rather than accede to demands for multiple orgasms.

Changing definitions of motherhood brought about changed definitions of fatherhood. And it was the strident feminists who decided what those changes were supposed to be. Father had to be brutally torn away from the *Wall Street Journal*, *True*, *Playboy*, and the television set and participate more fully in child care and household tasks, more commonly known as "shitwork" in the jargon of the feminist consciousness-raising groups of the early 1970s. Full equality would be automatically assured when men gladly (or otherwise) shared the yoke of "degradation" in child care.

Far from being condescendingly chucked under the chin as he labored hopelessly trying to fold a diaper, father was now expected to assume the role of male nursemaid in addition to his full-time occupation. He had to receive his comeuppance in his macho fantasies. Let Dad just once experience the exasperation of mud tracked onto a newly washed floor and the stranglehold of centuries of phallic imperialism would melt away.

With the advent of women's consciousness-raising groups, the rules of the fatherhood game were to change radically and drastically. From bumbling oaf who could not be trusted with either an aerosol spray household product or a potential spray baby, Dad was to transform himself magically into the greatest household applicance since the washer-dryer. Epithets were hurled at men in their father role as well as their employer role. The father role was undergoing a transformation from "hands off" to "hands on" where child care was concerned.

In the midst of this transition, along came the "men's movement."

The major question usually asked about the men's movement is, "Does it exist?" Yes, Virginia, it exists. The next question is, "What are its aims?" The answer to that question depends upon which movement leader you happen to be talking to at the moment and precisely what it is from which he wants to be liberated. Although smaller and much less known than the women's movement, the men's movement has at least as much divisiveness, dissent, and total disdain for disagreeing factions. As the aims of the women's movement can vary from having more women in top management in industry to complete overthrow of the government by violence and lesbian rule installed, so does the men's movement vary in its aims.

Warren Farrell, author of *The Liberated Man*, believes men should be liberated from role-deadlocking. Herb Goldberg, in his book, *The Hazards of Being Male: Surviving the Myth of Masculine Privilege*, believes that men ought to be liberated from women's liberation. New Yorkers are familiar with the sight of Harry Britton, who has taken up a post at Rockefeller Center, wearing signs with slogans such as, "Husband Lib. We Want Wives That OBEY . . . Down with Women's Lip." Some of the men's consciousness-raising groups have turned up some theories that have proven quite unsettling to some women. This faction appeals largely to dependent, passive men who would not object at all, thank you, to the idea of being supported by a woman (or anyone else, for that matter). Still others take the "anything-you-can-do, I-can-do-better" approach to male–female role-deadlocking. Win spoke to one leader of a men's rap group who assured her that he could bake a better banana bread than she could ever hope to. (He's probably right.)

The men's movement, such as it is, runs the gamut from "Take back your balls, fellows" to "Gracious me, we have been chauvinist pigs and we must stop it. At once!"

Marc Feingen Fasteau seems to be the superstar in this category. His book, *The Male Machine*, evokes the following reaction from Stephen Koch:

> Feigen Fasteau's book makes one wonder if it is even possible to speak at all accurately or honestly about the masculine experience from the feminist position. It also raises some severe questions about the character of the people who claim to be that movement's seers. Still, I can recommend *The Male Machine* to any man who fears that embracing feminism means abjection, self-hatred. For truly, this is no work of self-hatred. It is, on the contrary, one of the most complacent, self-admiring and snobbish books with any claim to seriousness I recall having

read. It claims to be a rich, deeply personal testament straight from the soul of Feminist Man.[5]

"Feminist Man," or "men's liberation" can provoke at least as much animosity from feminists as the "male chauvinist pig" can. Veronica Geng, in an article entitled "Requiem for the Women's Movement," has the following to say about the contribution to the feminist cause "From the soul of Feminist Man," in a section entitled "The Alibi of the 'Higher Cause.' ": "Human lib at its most reactionary has produced a joke called men's liberation (leading theoreticians, Marc Feigen Fasteau and Warren Farrell). . . . Men's libbers are colonial administrators whining about the malaria."[6]

But "men's lib" is under attack from still another source; Richard Doyle, whom we met in chapter 2, has the following indictment for the Feigen Fasteau/Farrell school of thought:

> The National Organization for Women is presently sponsoring a movement of semi-male turncoats to bleat the feminist party line. Pop sociologists, nouveau-liberals, and reluctant males of mixed sexual persuasion, they are thoroughly domesticated, housebroken creatures who hold their manhood cheap— apologetically, in fact. Denouncing their masculinity and pitifully groping at each other in "consciousness raising sessions," they hold men to be inferior beings. One probable motivation for those who happen to be hetrosexual [sic] is the prospect of easy sex from the amoral "libbers;" its [sic] probably not worth having however. It galls this writer that they presumptiously purport to represent "men's lib". True men's liberationists were around long before these tagtails ever felt the urge to slip into a pair of panties.[7]

Will the real men's movement please stand up?

The ivory tower school of the men's movement has some strong feelings about the fatherhood role. According to its adherents, not only are men capable of upstaging women in baking banana bread and folding diapers, but nurturing, cooing, soothing, and everything

5. Koch, "The Guilty Sex," p. 56.

6. Veronica Geng, "Requiem for the Women's Movement," *Harper's*, November 1976, p. 63.

7. R. F. Doyle, *The Rape of the Male* (St. Paul, Minn.: Poor Richard's Press, 1976), p. 167.

short of breast-feeding should be included in the Daddy repertory. Equality and "role-sharing" to them would create still another father image—the male madonna. As one of the arguments in the early days of the women's movement was that menstruation does not interfere with a woman's executive abilities, so would certain segments of the men's movement have us believe that possession of testicles does not automatically disqualify a man from kissing the booboo.

A startling discovery turned up during research of the segment of the men's movement advocating the male madonna image: None of its most eloquent spokepeople turned out to be fathers.

Within the span of one generation, the image of the ideal father has undergone a 180-degree turn, from bumbling fool who was not to interfere with the sacred rites of the female madonna to male madonna.

But remember, the foregoing described the role of the *married-*father of the 1950s and 1960s. Now let's take a jump ahead to the divorced father of the 1970s and the subsequent metamorphosis of his fatherhood role.

"Fatherhood meant delivering, or not delivering, checks."

You've come a long way, baby!

7

THE FATHER REALITY

The incident has reached legendary proportions in operatic circles. The terrified young baritone was auditioning before the most terrifying conductor in musical history. On top of that, the aria was the most famous baritone solo in the entire Italian repertoire, "Di Provenzal Mar," from Verdi's *La Traviata*. Besides its technical challenges, the dramatic implications were vast. The tearful father was imploring his son to leave the courtesan with whom he had been living and return to the serene family home in the provinces, bringing joy to his aging parents. The young singer trembled fearfully under the ominous glare of the conductor. However, he did his best as he sang the Italian words to:

> See your aging father here,
> Ah, what suffering he has known!

Maestro looked up contemptuously as he lowered his baton: "Are you a father?" he asked.

"No," the young singer croaked, rather than spoke.

"It sound it," replied Toscanini.

Robert Merrill survived the ordeal sufficiently to become not only a father but one of the world's leading operatic baritones as well.

We cite the incident that occurred in 1945 because to us it points out that Maestro Toscanini was every bit as proficient in his concept of fatherhood as in his concept of music.

Although the emotional significance of fatherhood has not received quite the same amount of attention as motherhood has, it has been there nevertheless, and its existence has been significant to fathers as well as to children. But even in the years when fatherhood was virtually forced underground, men felt their fatherhood identity, and to be cut off from it provoked reactions like the following from a newly divorced father:

> There were a thousand things he wanted to tell Jimmy, but he felt like a mute come to confession. He wanted to tell him he was frightened about a future that began when he left home: a future of furnished rooms and living on the cheap to support two households. . . . That he was worried that Jimmy would grow up and gradually become estranged. . . . [1]

While the importance of mother–child interaction has been spotlighted as being crucial to the development of both mother and child, father–child interaction, when mentioned at all, has usually been portrayed as, at best, a one-sided arrangement, of possible benefit to the child while being, simultaneously, a total inconvenience for the father. But our findings show that men were deeply involved with their fatherhood in spite of cultural denial of this aspect of manhood. The best example we heard about was from Pat, a visitation father who had tried (unsuccessfully) to see his son on his birthday. We asked this burly truck driver (who looked like a walking stereotype of studied macho cool) about his relationship with his children when they were babies.

"It's like this," he answered us. "When you pick up somebody's kid and the kid spits up on you, you worry about the shirt, right?"

"Right," answered Win.

"But when it's your own kid, you worry about the kid. Right?"

"Right," answered Ira.

Is fatherhood due for a renaissance? We have found bits and pieces of the importance of father involvement in child development—most of it, we must admit, in publications aimed toward a female readership.

Dr. Margaret A. Ribble, a child psychiatrist of some renown in the 1940s and 1950s, wrote *The Rights of Infants* in 1943. In her preface to the second edition, published in 1965, she has the following to say:

1. Charles Howe, "Weekend Father," *The Future of the Family,* Louise Kapp Howe, ed. (New York: Simon & Schuster, 1972), p. 114.

Little has been added to this new edition except for increased emphasis in . . . the role of the father in the early personal adjustment of the young child to an understanding of maleness and femaleness, which can become a life problem. . . .[2]

The lack of emphasis on the father's role in child development was not lost on Dr. Ribble:

So much has been said about the mothering of an infant, it might well be inferred that the role of the father in the early life of his child is negligible. . . . The lack of a father relationship early in life can leave a painful gap in a child's feelings. One of the most important impressions of an infant, even in his early months, is the experience that there are two sorts of people in the world. . . .[3]

Robert Coles, a psychiatrist noted for his liberation from Freudian dogma, had the following to say abut father–child involvement when he was asked, in a 1973 magazine interview, what he saw as the function of a father in a family: "The same as the function of a mother. To give his children affection and support. To set standards."[4]

While most child psychiatrists, when discussing father–child interaction, are concerned primarily with its effect on children, other concerned humanists and sociologists are equally concerned with the effects on fathers of an impaired relationship: Under the heading of "Missing: The Concept of Fatherhood," Myron Benton says:

Seen in the light of learned maternal behavior, American males are on the whole woefully short-changed when it comes to learning and being encouraged to learn their paternal roles. Preparation for motherhood is a cumulative experience. It starts in very early childhood and is progressively reinforced until the girl actually becomes a mother. By comparison, men are clearly disadvantaged in their preparation for fatherhood. Since their potential for the paternal role isn't structured by a biological

2. Margaret A. Ribble, *The Rights of Infants*, 2nd ed., (New York: Columbia University Press, 1965), p. v.

3. Ibid., p. 90.

4. Rollie Hochstein, "An Interview with Child Psychiatrist Robert Coles," *Family Circle*, November 1973, p. 76.

framework, boys ought to be made especially cognizant of the multifarious parental responses they'll be called on to exhibit one day. Instead, they see—in their own homes—that fatherhood either assumes narrow dimensions or is more or less irrelevant. They don't get the feel of fatherhood the way a girl gets it for motherhood. The result is that, as psychoanalyst Bruno Bettelheim has said, "Only very occasionally, for boys, is fatherhood added like an afterthought as part of their self-image as mature men."[5]

The American man never had his Dr. Spock championing his cause or reminding him how essential interaction with his child was for both his own and his child's development. But one researcher, Dr. Henry B. Biller, of the University of Rhode Island, did not let the importance of the father role escape him or his research. His book, *Father, Child and Sex Role: Paternal Determinants of Personality Development*, is regarded as one of the classics is this neglected field. He states: "The father is a model for his child. His positive involvement facilitates the boy's cognitive functioning, his ability to control his impulses and to function independently and responsibly, and his overall interpersonal competence."[6]

David B. Lynn of the University of California is another researcher concerned with the father role. In his book, *The Father: His Role in Child Development*, he has the following to say:

> A close father–child relationship is more often associated with a cohesive family that holds positive values than a close mother–child relationship. Fathers are usually more punitive and stricter than mothers, although mothers may use a wider variety of punishments. Fathers frequently perceive their role as vital to the child's development, but some seem, nevertheless, to take insufficient advantage of the time available to them to spend with their child.[7]

But it was not until 1974 that father, per se, was spotlighted as a parent in a book directed especially toward him, rather than toward

5. Myron Benton, "The Paradox of the American Father," *The Future of the Family*, Louise Kapp Howe, ed. (New York: Simon & Schuster, 1972), p. 127.

6. Henry B. Biller, *Father, Child and Sex Role: Paternal Determinants of Personality Development* (Lexington, Mass.: Heath, Lexington Books, 1971), p. 33.

7. David B. Lynn, *The Father: His Role in Child Development* (Monterey, Calif.: Brooks/Cole Publishing Co., 1974), pp. 238, 239.

researchers and psychologists. *Father Power* by Henry Biller and Dennis Meredith (McKay, 1974) is seemingly the first book directed toward fathers which regards fatherhood as a unique aspect of a man's life with beneficial results for both fathers and children.

Unfortunately, the father role is rarely scrutinized until the father leaves the picture. While the father role has been given some credit in relation to teen-age sons, primarily to avert homosexuality, psychologists Edith Atkin and Estelle Rubin, in their book, *Part-Time Father*, have given us an overview of the father role in different stages of child development. From the "Father and Infant" section: "Fathers enhance the baby's experience with a contact that differs from what the mother provides. . . . Daddy looks different, sounds different, smells different. . . . A baby needs to hear a deep voice, to sense the way a man handles a child."[8]

In describing the father's relationship to the preschool child: "Just as childhood is a period of development and maturation, so fatherhood is an evolving role. As changes occur in the child, there are accompanying shifts in the father's functioning in order to meet the child's different needs."[9]

If there is a dearth of printed matter on the father–child relationship in a conventional, two-parent home, father does get spotlighted in a negative way once he leaves the home. He is rarely referred to as the father. Rather, he is the missing element in expressions like "broken home," "one-parent home," "single-parent home," or "children of divorce." All of these expressions imply father absence. The crucial point here is that the question, "What effect will the divorce have on the children?" can be rephrased to ask, "What effect, if any, will father absence have on children?" (We will discuss this more fully in chapter 10.) It is rarely, if ever, asked, "What effect will child deprivation have on a father?"

The father–child relationship, especially in the early years, has simply never been glorified in either literature or art. We have no poetry describing the father–child bond other than the brimstone and hellfire connotations of the Oedipal mess. We do, however, have letters from fathers who tell us what father–child interaction means to them and what child deprivation can do to a father. The following letter was sent to the director of a divorced father's group asking about his chances of obtaining custody:

8. Edith Atkin and Estelle Rubin, *Part-Time Father: A Guide for the Divorced Father* (New York: Vanguard Press, 1976), p. 31.
    9. Ibid., p. 35.

My wife is a very ambitious person with a successful career in psychiatric social work. She has always worked during our eighteen years of marriage and she makes more money than I do. I teach at the University of _____ and have always been less ambitious than my wife wanted me to be. My working hours were fewer and more flexible, and, in effect, I became the person who took care of the boys and the home. And I liked doing this. The family became the center of my life. My wife, on the other hand, became more heavily involved with her career, taking on extra activities to the extent that she had almost no time and energy left for me and the boys and the home. She began to resent my time with the children and began to have nothing but contempt for me as a man. This led to her forcing me to get out.

Since I left home she has cut down on her activities very little, if any. She is not able to keep up the place very well. I am beginning to feel that it would be better if I had custody of the boys. Their ages are eight, ten, and twelve. But I have heard that it is very difficult for fathers to get custody, even joint custody, of their children.

Another father, in a plea to the family relations office handling his case, writes the following:

I have had no reply from your office since my letter to you of [dated one year previously] in which I informed you of the complete breakdown of communications with my children, J_____ and C_____, since their move to Arizona. You then agreed that my former wife was obviously in contempt of court, but could do nothing, as Arizona was out of the [home state] court's jurisdiction.

This March I received a letter from my daughter and a second one in June informing me of her school grades, a picture, etc. I also received a letter from my son last month. This was the first communication with the children in over two and one-half years. I have not been able to call them as you know, due to the fact that my former wife instructed you not to give out her phone number, which she keeps unlisted. Even though the court ordered her to have the children call me collect once a month she has forbidden them to call or have any contact with me or their grandparents.

Since reading my daughter's second letter, I have strong

doubts that she received my reply, and it would appear that their mother censors all mail and passes on only what she wants them to receive. However, their strong indication of wanting to see me this summer (copies of letters enclosed) and my daughter's letter of last month prompted me to call them at their [maternal] grandmother's house, where they were staying. I tried to call them this morning, but Mrs. R_____ [the maternal grandmother] advised me to contact my lawyer if I wanted to see the children. . . . I admit that I had given my ex-wife the benefit of the doubt and had hoped that with age perhaps she had gained a little maturity and had reconsidered so that we could, after all this time, work out an amicable agreement for all concerned. I'm sure she was well aware of the letters the children wrote and their expression of a desire to visit with me this summer *if even only for a lunch* [italics ours].

My former wife has been in contempt of court, yet nothing is done. My former case worker at Family Relations, L.W., with whom I have had contact and who is now at the T_____ facility, has voiced his opinion that my former wife is impossible to deal with and that I received a raw deal because no one is willing to become involved. Her former attorney has expressed the same sentiments, yet Family Relations Court still chooses to ignore any plea for a fair hearing.

The divorced father's movement knows what the father role is. They know it because they're trying to fulfill it in spite of what often seem to be insurmountable odds. Most of its members do not look to "experts" to define the role for them, nor are they particularly perturbed that it is an aspect of human development that has been largely ignored in the mountains of child-care literature that has stressed the mother role to the seeming exclusion of all other human relations. They are, however, perturbed that this father role, if acknowledged at all, is completely overlooked or denied by the courts of law. They are fighting mad. And they are fighting. They are fighting for the right to be functioning fathers. Some of them, like the father in the second letter, are fighting for the right to telephone their children. Others, like the father in our first letter, are fighting for complete custody.

The divorced fathers' movement is vague, scattered, and at this point largely uncoordinated. It is not to be confused with the men's movement which we discussed in the previous chapter, primarily because these men do not have to join consciousness-raising groups to find out what it means to be men. They know that fatherhood is an essential component of manhood. It would be difficult to assess their membership, as groups come and go. In Appendix A we have attempted to list those which we feel have a core of stability. It should be noted, however, that many fathers are fighting with no group affiliation. Their aims vary from getting laws changed to getting them enforced where visitation is concerned.

Currently, efforts to organize these groups nationally are being made, primarily by Divorced Men of Connecticut and the National Center for Child Custody Information (see Appendix A). Some of these groups recommend lawyers known for their interest and success in father-custody cases, some help their members fight *pro se*, i.e., without legal representation. If you're reminded of the saying "He who represents himself in court has a fool for a lawyer and a fool for a client," try to bear in mind that most of these men have had very costly, disappointing, and unsuccessful experiences with lawyers, such as the father who wrote the following letter to a divorced father's group:

> If the tone of this letter seems uncertain, it is because since October 15, 1974, I have found out that I have no rights as an individual. Since that date I have been told that I am no longer entitled to a husband's, father's or human rights. I have found out that I have been cheated, lied to and legally abused. Even though I have a lawyer who is understanding, he tells me that I must learn that I have no rights. My three children, ages seven through eleven don't want to live with their mother any longer; they have told the court and the court-appointed psychologist that they would prefer to live with me. Still, I understand that my chances of winning my custody suit are about one in fifty.
>
> If, in any way, you can give me assistance or direction, please give me a call or write me as I realize that soon after the next court appearance I must become an outlaw if I wish to maintain a real place in my children's lives.

Emotional support is indicated for these fathers at least as much as legal advice and assistance. These groups have quite a few women members—second wives (see chapter 16), sisters, and mothers of divorced men, as well as divorced mothers who feel that their former husbands are not quite that saintly as fathers.

Another reason that they are not heard from very much in the media as a "rights" group is the lack of time necessary to organize. Most of them have a sense of immediacy in their own cases. Another major factor that must be taken into consideration is that these men are often employed in demanding and time-consuming jobs, many of them holding down two jobs in order to meet court-ordered alimony and support payments for children they are not permitted to see. Most of the various "rights" groups are made up largely of the overeducated and underemployed, who can devote their time and energy to marches, demonstrations, and press coverage of their cause. Also, the divorced fathers' movement does have its fanatic fringe, which makes the moderate core wary of mass amalgamation and demonstrations.

Most of these men are fighting not only for fathers' rights and children's representation in court but against ingrained attitudes of a man's lack of fitness in the child-raising role as well.

Although the women's movement has prescribed various and sundry alternatives for that damnation of modern-day life, the nuclear family, it has never occurred to them to suggest the father-headed, one-parent family. Says Maureen Green: "In the general shake-up that marriage and the family are undergoing at present, the prophets and activists are all pointing to the death of the family as the way ahead; other groups, be it commune or kibbutz, are envisioned that will help the individual survive better."[10]

In addition to the laboratory-fertilized and developed fetus, the commune, as the replacement for the nuclear family, has been most frequently hailed as the saviour of women from the double curse of childbearing and child-raising. As with other proclamations of the more righteously adamant fringe of the women's movement, father's opinions have rarely been solicited, especially when that fringe declared the father role obsolete in child-rearing as well as fertilization. Or, to quote one father in our sampling, "That shmuck, who asked him?"

Bill Ralston (more about him in chapter 11) writes us of his experience with alternatives to the nuclear family:

On March 8, 1973, my wife, Susan E. Ralston, left our home in Olean, New York, with our two young children, Marc Allan,

10. Maureen Green, *Fathering* (New York: McGraw-Hill, 1976), p. 11.

then age 4, and Shari Lynn, then age 3, to live in a commune in Massachusetts. After I made several trips to this commune unsuccessfully attempting to reason with her and convince her to return to our home with our children, I then petitioned the courts for custody to retrieve our children from this unstable, squalid communal lifestyle and environment. In September, 1973, the court ordered my wife to remove our children from this commune and return them to our home pending a final divorce and custody trial scheduled for December 1973. The court was not very favorable towards her lifestyle and my wife suspected she would not be granted custody. She then took matters into her own hands by intentionally violating the court's orders and on October 8, 1973, with the help of the Massachusetts commune people, absconded our two children and disappeared with them prior to our pending divorce and custody trial. I was subsequently granted custody of our two children, but have been left with no effective legal recourse to locate and recover my children.

Initially, I thought surely there must be legal recourses that would help me to locate my children and enforce the court's orders. Many months later, after incurring thousands of dollars in legal fees and private investigators' fees, I realized there were no legal recourses to help me. I was quite dismayed when the judge told me, "Our courts can only render court orders, but we cannot enforce them interstate." My custody order seemingly is not worth the paper it is written on.

Ralston subsequently founded UPAC—United Parents of Absconded Children. Although he has not yet located Marc and Shari, he reports that as of this writing, he has successfully found and recovered children for twenty-one parents who have been awarded custody.

He sounds like a father to us.

8

THE DILEMMA OF
THE DIVORCED FATHER:
THE DARK SIDE
OF EQUAL RIGHTS

In Utopia all divorced mothers recognize the children's need
for contact with their fathers.[1]

The dilemma of the divorced father is easy to describe: He is faced
with the choice of being either a functioning father or a law-abiding
citizen. In Utopia he can be both. In reality he often ends up as
neither.

All divorces are not made in heaven. However, the rise in the
divorce rate has given way to a rise in advice on "How to achieve a
happy divorce," or, as one friend of ours describes it: "Divorce
advice: from drek to dross."

As we have mentioned before, according to June and William
Noble, "Custody means control. It means ownership, power,
authority."[2] In their book, *Uncoupling: The Art of Coming Apart*,
authors Norman Sheresky and Marya Mannes blithely assure us:

> Of course, the granting of custody to one parent or another
> does not give the custodial parent exclusive rights over the
> welfare of the child. . . . She [the mother] cannot choose the
> child's school or make other major decisions without consulting
> the husband. The court, if it must intervene, will arbitrate the
> parties' major differences and direct what is best for the child.

1. Edith Atkin and Estelle Rubin, *Part-Time Father* (New York: Vanguard Press,
1976), p. 117.
2. June and William Noble, *The Custody Trap* (New York: Hawthorn Books, 1975),
p. 69.

Ordinarily, however, the court will not interfere in the *rational* [italics ours] decision of the parent who has custody.[3]

But, to most divorced fathers (and to us) the most ominous advice from the experts comes from no less hallowed sources than Joseph Goldstein, professor of law at Yale; Anna Freud, daughter of Sigmund; and Albert J. Solnit, director of the Child Study Center at Yale:

> As in adoption a custody decree would be final, that is, not subject to modification. . . . In addition, certain conditions such as visitations may themselves be a source of discontinuity. . . . A "visiting" or "visited" parent has little chance to serve as a true object for love. . . . Once it is determined who will be the custodial parent, it is that parent, *not the court*, who must decide under what conditions he or she wishes to raise the child. Thus, *the noncustodial parent should have no legally enforceable right to visit the child, and the custodial parent should have the right to decide whether it is desirable for the child to have such visits* [italics ours].[4]

No matter what the conflicting theories are, the criteria a divorced father will have to live up to in order to be regarded as law-abiding are very simple: "Roll over, play dead, pay up."

Following is the dilemma of one divorced father who tried to function as a participating parent. This incident is excerpted from the *Court Watcher*, the monthly newsletter of the Divorced Men's Association of Connecticut. A DMAC member, denied visitation in spite of court orders to the contrary, wrote to the school board in 1974 requesting copies of his children's school records. This request was granted until November 25, 1975, when the school board advised him:

> We have been requested by Mrs. B———, now that the divorce has become final and she has been awarded custody of the children, that we discontinue sending you any reports regarding them. The request was referred to our school district

3. Norman Sheresky and Marya Mannes, *Uncoupling: The Art of Coming Apart* (New York: Viking Press, 1972), p. 143.

4. Joseph Goldstein, Anna Freud, and Albert J. Solnit, *Beyond the Best Interests of the Child* (New York: Free Press, 1973), pp. 37, 38.

counsel and I am enclosing a copy of his reply for your information.[5]

The letter from the school system's legal counsel reads as follows:

I have reviewed the questions concerning the B_____ children and find that the School District is no longer responsible for providing grades and reports to the father. Since Mrs. B_____ has custody of the children all correspondence and contact concerning the children should be made with her. Therefore I suggest that the decision to notify the father concerning discipline problems and grades should be reversed.[6]

The father in question has long ago given up any pretense at being a law-abiding citizen where his parental role is concerned.

Henry is a model divorced father where the courts are concerned. He has been doing the "Roll over, play dead, pay up" number since his divorce three years ago, keeping his two children in an exclusive New York City private school. Henry has admitted to us that he never was that much of a father even during his marriage, and he makes no bones about resenting his "male Nanny" role on Sundays now.

Henry had a different dilemma regarding his daughter, Valerie's, school problem. His former wife called him with the message, "*Your daughter* is having problems in school." Henry went down to speak to the headmistress, because his wife "did not want to be bothered." The discussion lasted four hours.

Thirteen-year-old Valerie had every problem a child could have—poor scholastic performance, inability to get along with others, disruptiveness in class—but most disturbing to school officials was that she would disappear without explanation, and neither the school nor her mother knew where she was. Henry was told that the school would have to expel Valerie; they could not take the responsibility. As the headmistress told Henry: "Her mother doesn't care about her; her stepfather [sic] resents her. She needs a stable home environment and she isn't getting it. This is New York City and she could turn too easily to drugs and the streets."

He asked her if she thought Valerie would do better living with him and was relieved when the headmistress said no. She emphasized

5. *Court Watcher* (Waterbury, Conn.), 1, No. 9 (November 1976): 3.
6. Ibid.

that Valerie needed a stable home environment with constant supervision. Henry told her he would speak to Valerie's maternal grandparents, and perhaps she could go and live with them in England, but the headmistress expressed doubt that two older people could undertake the responsibility of a severely disturbed teen-ager. Henry was also aware that her grandparents, as well as his own family, "couldn't stand" Valerie.

He described the headmistress as a mature, understanding woman, genuinely concerned with Valerie, whom she described as an "unusually bright, alert girl." She felt the solution rested in Henry's discussing the situation seriously with his ex-wife.

"How could I tell her," Henry asks with a shake of his head, "that every time I try to talk to Margot about Valerie all she ever says is, 'I'm not interested in the problems that you created with *your daughter*,' and hangs up the phone?" He is looking for neither self-justification, blame-shifting, nor pity. He has dutifully paid for private psychiatric care for both children since the divorce. He admits that he is afraid to think about Valerie.

There was a time when the "Roll over, play dead, pay up" approach provided some balm to the father's sense of guilt. When the feminine mystique held sway, he could have consoled himself that his disappearing act was, indeed, "in the best interests of the child." Brainwashed into believing himself to be a bumbling fool in the parent role, he could rationalize that his absence would insure a conflict-free future for his children as well as his wife. His competence as a father would have been in direct proportion to the comforts and luxuries he could provide for his children.

It was simply assumed that mother custody would guarantee the children's well-being. But the implications of the sexual revolution and "liberation" for women regarding the motherhood role were not lost on the divorced father. Time and again, the divorced mother was encouraged not to let the presence of her children act as a deterrent to her "fulfillment."

Jared is my boyfriend, or lover, or man-I'm-involved-with, or man-I-love, or whatever one's supposed to say these days. . . . Not that the arrangement I have with Jared is unusual, at least by the standards of my neighborhood. . . . Anyhow, Jared spends plenty of time at the house, and that particular morning I'd forgotten to lock the bedroom door. Sara, who's eight, walked in, saw our two bodies under the covers, and said, "Hey, Ma! What's Jared doing on top of you?"[7]

Quite a few noncustodial fathers would be very grateful if only one Jared were on top of his children's custodial mother. Still others feel that their former wives are entitled to a normal sex life and do not believe that a child walking in unannounced will necessarily be traumatized for the rest of his or her life. What concerns them is the studied, offhand casualness regarding the "swinging" or "liberated" life-style. The dilemma of these fathers is that they are reluctant to label their wives "unfit," as they are reluctant to plead their cause as male madonnas or argue about whether or not a paternal instinct exists.

One of the changes that has been brought about by the women's movement is that many men, albeit reluctantly at first, took on more responsibility in household and child-care chores, developing closer ties with their children in the process.

Equal rights for father? The following is quoted from a lawyer's convention in a section entitled "Custody for Fathers?":

> Harry Fain [an attorney] took the view that because it is such an uphill fight when one represents the father that it is important to have sound psychiatric testimony. He had a case in which a *very impressive psychiatrist* witness showed that to the child involved the *real* parent was definitely the father. You must try in such a case to get psychiatric testimony that the child needs the father, and will be devastated if deprived of him [italics ours].[8]

Joseph Epstein, in *Divorced in America*, has this to say about equal rights for fathers:

> As is fairly common knowledge, the situation [of a father automatically being given custody, as was prevalent in England in 1765] has been exactly reversed, and today in matters of custody it is the mother whose position under the law has become dominant. Whereas under common law a father's unfitness as a person was insufficient cause for him to be denied

7. Colette Dowling, "Liberation Breeds Rotten Kids," *Cosomopolitan*, November 1976, p. 174.

8. *Family Law Reporter*, 2 FLR 2688, 17 August, 1976.

custody of his children—he had to be shown unfit as a parent, a very different thing as the law understood it, and understands it still—so now the same case must be made against a woman who, if she is to be denied custody of her children in a divorce action, must be shown to be not merely inadequate as a parent or person but, in the language of one legal writer, "so depraved, immoral, and wicked that to allow the child to remain in the mother's custody would be harmful to its best interests."[9]

Are we therefore to assume that all a custody-desirous father has to do is prove that his wife is "so depraved, immoral and wicked . . ."? Once she is so proven, will the father automatically be awarded custody? Not the father who came to Ira's group for consultation. His former wife was, admittedly, a prostitute whose pimp baby-sat for her while she plied her trade. His lawyer told him there was "nothing he could do." A favorite story goes around one divorced fathers' group about a trial where there was evidence that a custodial mother had been into the "depraved, immoral and wicked" scene for two years, with gory evidence submitted dating to two months prior to the trial itself.

"And for the last two months?" the judge asked the father's lawyer.

"We have no evidence of the last two months, Your Honor," answered the lawyer.

"Amazing," answered His Honor. "In just two months' time this little lady has seen the error of her ways and has transformed herself from the Whore of Babylon into Snow White."

The father who lost the case doesn't think it's quite so funny.

The reluctance of the courts to consider father as a possible alternative to mother, even in horrific cases of child abuse, is beyond the understanding of divorced fathers, and their protests are beginning to receive sympathetic attention from a wider public. In a Boston paper, three members of Fathers United for Equal Justice cited the case of a three-year-old girl who was given into her mother's custody by a judge. After one year in her mother's care, the child had suffered food poisoning and broken limbs, and was living in home conditions of filth and cruelty. She was finally rescued and placed in a hospital by her father.

9. Joseph Epstein, *Divorced in America* (New York: E. P. Dutton, 1974), pp. 189, 190.

> When social workers and a psychiatrist had succeeded in persuading the court to take custody away from the mother, the child was then unaccountably placed in a foster home.[10]

Unaccountably is the key word in virtually all cases when custody is denied the father where the custodial mother is proven unfit beyond all reasonable doubt.

What about the father who has neither intention nor desire of proving his wife "so depraved, immoral and wicked," yet wishes that the "liberated" custodial mother would close the bedroom door once in a while? What about the father whose former wife is not "so depraved, immoral or wicked," who conducts her personal life at least reasonably discreetly, does not inflict atrocities on the child, and is an adequate mother? And he wants to be more than a Sunday Santa. His dilemma may be the greatest of all. He has to prove himself capable of parenthood in spite of his maleness.

This is the thrust of the moderate core of the divorced fathers' movement. From visitation rights to complete custody, the fathers' chances represent the dark side of equal rights. There was a faint glimmer of hope that they would have the cooperation of the women's movement in the early 1970s, but the movement has become increasingly hostile to divorced men, especially fathers. It is interesting to note that virtually every faction of the divorced men's and divorced fathers' movements, from ultraright to ultraliberal, supported the Equal Rights Amendment. It is equally interesting to note that one of the major scare tactics of anti-ERA women's groups was the warning that passage of the ERA could mean fathers having an equal chance at child custody.

Unfortunately, antifeminist feeling runs high among fathers' rights groups. We say "unfortunately" because so much of the proposed reform, such as children's representation in court and joint custody, is emanating from feminist lawyers. The antagonism of the right-wing faction is understandable when we stop to think that these men are still living by the "*kinde, küche, kirche*" or "keep 'em pregnant and barefoot" philosophy. This faction wants to see women punished after a divorce, and most of them are fighting more for elimination of child-support payments than for custody.

The more educated or higher socioeconomic faction of the divorced fathers' movement is embittered at the women's movement

10. Maureen Green, *Fathering,* (New York: McGraw-Hill, 1976), pp. 117, 118.

because, as one divorced doctor put it, "The movement doesn't put its movements where its mouth is." These men couldn't care less about "punishing" their wives following a divorce, as evidence has shown them time and again that the better the former wife's post-divorce adjustment, the better the chance she will voluntarily relinquish custody. Some fathers admit to a dilemma where the women's movement is concerned. One says "The point is, our (or my) chauvinism is more personal than broad-based. My mind says that I believe in equality but my head says that equality is not what these women are looking for. The women's movement, in all fairness, has endorsed father custody and, on occasion, joint custody, but only where it has been instigated by the mother."

Divorced fathers' groups have the support of women as well, especially those women who feel that certain factions of the women's movement are, on occasion, carrying things too far. Following are excerpts from a letter written by a woman to a director of a divorced fathers' group in response to a NOW Father's Day demonstration ("Give Dad a Subpoena for Father's Day"):

> The father's only legal rights to his children are financial. The emotional day-to-day contacts with his children are not con-sidered in a divorce, and more often than not the children are used as pawns by the mothers to collect support payments.
>
> Who is to say that a child is better off with the mother? Why should the father have to pay a ridiculous amount of money for the "privilege" of seeing his own children one day a week?
>
> Women are crying for equal rights, but are they willing to accept the responsibilities such rights would bring? Where are men's rights in a divorce action?
>
> I ask the women of NOW, and all women, what would you do if you were faced with paying a great deal of money to a man who had hurt you deeply, for the privilege of seeing your own children for a few hours each week? Your choices would be to pay, go to jail, or run.

The financial aspect of divorce has been the most explosive issue since divorce increased in the middle class. Formerly, divorce was most prevalent in the higher income brackets, where supporting two households was not a major problem, and the lowest income brackets, where the father rarely supported the family during the marriage. The truth of the matter is that two households cannot be maintained as cheaply as one. The woman who has been accustomed to living at the $60,000-per-year.level will feel just as deprived when she is forced to live on half that amount as the woman accustomed to living at the $15,000-a-year level. The women's media, both the traditional, service-oriented and the more militant publications, increasingly point out the "victim" status of the divorced mother: "America's four million divorcees are the new poor of our society. If last year's divorce rate holds steady, they will be joined by at least another million in 1976, swelling the ranks of women and children who once lived in middle-class comfort and who now live in or near hardship and poverty."[11]

The question of who gets raked over the coals more in a divorce settlement is, oddly enough, not as explosive between men and women as it is between women and women. Resentment, understandably, runs high among second wives who have worked all their adult lives and, upon marrying, find most of their income going to support first wives' "middle-class comfort." A second wife voices her resentment over the demands of a first wife:

> She was awarded $45.00 per week alimony (no minor children involved) on the first $100 per week that my husband earns on commissions and 1/3 of all dollars above that, not to exceed $95.00 per week for three years, and $25.00 per week for the next two years. Not much incentive to work hard at selling real estate, is there? This award was made while he was collecting unemployment.
>
> Since then the real estate business has dropped off considerably. As a result, an arrearage of $3,600. Our understanding is that the court does not care where you get the money—just get it or else! My husband's income last year was $6,200—based on that, he can't get a loan—not even exist as a human being. May I add that she is thirty-eight years old and healthy but won't work.
>
> A man doesn't stand a chance in court against a woman. He gets taken to the cleaners and raked over the coals all at once. No wonder husbands are leaving the state. I would leave the state also.

11. Alice Lake, "Divorcées: The New Poor," *McCall's*, September 1976, p. 18.

The threat of a jail sentence is a reality for every *law-abiding* divorced father, no matter what the reasons may be for falling in arrears. It has been pointed out that technically, laws in most states threaten jail sentences for custodial mothers who have deprived fathers of court-ordered visitation rights. We have yet to hear of an instance of such a sentence enforced. This is not merely the judge's reluctance to incarcerate a mother. It is, at least in part, the father's reluctance to press for prosecution and its inevitable consequences for the children. Besides, most divorced fathers do not want to see their ex-wives in jail. They want to see their children.

9

COPPING OUT
AND DROPPING OUT

COPPING OUT

Phil Tierney, a father of three, said he was "representing the fathers without custody, who are often labeled 'the heavies.' " He described the difficulties of a separation, and their temptation to "cop out" and move away.

He also described the problem of the "recreational director syndrome," in which the father tries to entertain the children. Once past these hurdles, the non-custodial father still has the opportunity to "develop a relationship with his children that is permanent," that will last even after they are adults, he said.[1]

Tierney was referring to one form of "copping out" by divorced fathers—the most prevalent form. This is the law-abiding citizen, the ideal divorced father who will "roll over, play dead, pay up." He is not describing the full-desertion father, whom we will discuss later. He is referring to the divorced father who is taking the easiest way out in fulfilling the definition of "responsible father" according to the law. He is paying all the expenses of his children's upbringing, attempting to ease his guilt at the psychoemotional expense of his children's well-being. Often, this copping out represents the only way he can deal with his own emotional conflict.

1. Kathleen Kujawa, "Conference Highlights Problems of Divorced," *Divorce* (Newsletter of North American Conference of Separated and Divorced Catholics) March–April 1976, p. 3.

"By the time of the follow-up, Alex's clinical picture was one of a consolidated childhood depression. He was spending several pathetic hours each day rocking in his chair while listening quietly to phonograph records left by his father, and making repeated attempts to contact his father on his toy telephone."[2]

Over and over again, the advice is repeated: "Refrain from voicing criticism of the other parent. It is difficult but absolutely necessary for a child's healthy development. It is important that the child respect both parents."[3]

Many divorced fathers have no illusions about their ex-wives "refraining from voicing criticism." Some of the finer points of visitation roulette are not always detailed in the women's service magazines' portrayal of the victimized divorced mother. It is, like a father's chances of obtaining custody or, even being a fit parent, simply not mentioned. We did, however, come across one article in which a divorced mother warns others that indulging in visitation roulette could possibly backfire:

> She lists the various "tricks" she has observed:
>
> Insisting on maintaining the regular visiting day even though the husband's work schedule makes it impossible for him to come at that time.
>
> Explaining that the child or children cannot go out with the father because of illness or other plans made by the child.
>
> When the father arrives, the child is not dressed to go out, or is dirty and badly dressed—a trick to humiliate the ex-husband.
>
> Refusal to let a child talk to the father on the phone, or listening to the conversation. Some mothers, when they know a phone call is coming, tell the child what he or she should say and what he cannot mention. Sometimes a mother will force a child to lie to his father and stand by during the conversation to be sure her will is enacted.
>
> Refusal to let the child live with his father, even when he is able to give the child advantages and comforts the mother cannot provide. She has seen instances where even after a child has run away to go to his father, the courts and social workers upheld the mother.

2. Judith S. Wallerstein and Joan B. Kelly, "The Effects of Parental Divorce," *Journal of the American Academy of Child Psychiatry*, 14, No. 4 (Autumn 1975): 604.
3. *Parents Are Forever* (pamphlet), Washington, D.C.: Parents Without Partners.

> She goes on to say that although there are impossible and unreasonable fathers, many women are only hurting themselves by treating their ex-husbands as pariahs and punishing them through the children . . . they only lose their children by using them to get back at their ex-husbands. . . . In many cases, they [the children] have their own revenge by deserting their mothers and attempting to get in touch with their fathers. . . . These poor, benighted women often end up as Old Ladies Alone—divorced not only by their husbands but also by their children.[4]

The above excerpt is one of the rare examples we have seen of a custodial mother advised not to vilify the children's father because it may eventually backfire on her. But vilification of the noncustodial father is widespread.

Even in situations where visitation is based on full cooperation between divorced parents, the psychic wounds can cut deep. Men see themselves becoming more and more "incidental" in the lives of their children, especially those who were "absentee fathers" during the marriage. But for the man who had close involvement with his children prior to the divorce, visiting the home that was once his, seeing the garden and improvements that he may have built himself, realizing that he is often living in a furnished room to maintain his former wife and children in the life-style to which they have become accustomed can only increase the feeling of helplessness in a man who prides himself on his sense of responsibility.

Reams have been written about the divorced father who abandons his children financially. In fact, this is the stereotype of the divorced father, and he is always cited as the rule rather than the exception. Psychological abandonment on the part of the father is at least as detrimental to the child, but current divorce laws not only ignore this aspect of divorced father responsibility but encourage it in ways subtle and not so subtle. In making property settlements, providing a place for the children in the father's home is never taken into consideration. Many fathers are ashamed to take their children into their one-room apartment with a few sticks of furniture. Others, like Dave, who are not ashamed, tell us, "I live in one room. My kids are five, seven, and eleven. They go crazy in about an hour in my place."

Craig lives alone in the five-room apartment his family used to

---

4. Isabella Taves, "Woman Alone: Divorced Mothers Asking for Trouble," *The Western* (Litchfield, Conn.), 3 September, 1975.

share. He calls it a tomb. He has been keeping up the apartment for the two weeks a year his children spend with him. He knows the children are thriving well in the country town where they live with their mother and grandparents. He can afford to visit his children about once in six weeks, and they greet him enthusiastically when they see him. He is also confident that Karen, his former wife, will never vilify him to the children.

"Those kids were my entire life," he tells us. "I can't come home to this tomb every night and cry every time I inadvertently come across one of their books or toys."

Craig is considering a one-room bachelor apartment in a predominately singles' area. His friends have told him that he will have to build a new life for himself; he cannot go on brooding forever. His depression will not help him or his children. His friends have told him that he is luckier than most—he has the consolation that his children are thriving and think the world of him. He knows that a one-room apartment will mean the end of the children's week-long visits with him.

"But," he explains, "I've got to look at this thing realistically. I will never have the relationship with the children I once had. I couldn't ask for custody knowing that the children are doing better where they are."

Pierce doesn't want to be a cop-out father either. His former wife has been playing visitation roulette with his two daughters for the past five years and is now trying to have his visitation rights revoked altogether. His daughter called him "on the sneak" two months ago from a friend's house, but when he tried to call her at home, his wife curtly informed him, "Jennifer doesn't want to have anything to do with you."

He came to a divorced fathers' meeting to find out if there was any way he could get his two daughters into therapy.

"Even if I never see them until they're grown," he explains, "I want them to be able to have healthy relationships with men."

Pierce was advised to get some form of help for himself and stop spending weekends hoping his former wife would get a sudden attack of parental responsibility.

"Assert yourself as a man," a group member tells him. "Live like a man. Your daughters will come around when they've grown up."

"Hang in there," Richard advises.

Richard's three children are past custodial age. "You see them emerge as thinking, self-respecting people. They're ready to regard you as a human being, albeit an imperfect one. One day you're no longer the bastard their mother made you out to be. It's worth it. Resist the temptation when they're small to tell them their mother lied about you. It's too much of a trip to lay on them. Hang in there," he implores.

"What guarantee do we have that all we have to do is roll over, play dead, and pay up and some day our kids will see that we're really not such a son of a bitch after all?" asks Bob.

"None," Richard admits. "None whatsoever."

The temptation to cop out is strong enough when a divorced father sees himself as an unwanted extra in the growth and development of his children and when, like Craig, he has the consolation that his children are thriving in spite of his cipher status in their lives. Not all divorced fathers have that consolation, though.

There is one aspect of the courts labeling one parent the "fit" parent that has not been explored. That is, the fit custodial parent at the time of the divorce may not be quite that fit six months later, especially if he or she has not been able to cope with the postdivorce adjustment. Wallerstein and Kelly astutely make the connection between an unsatisfactory postdivorce adjustment and a breakdown of the parental functioning:

> Our overall findings . . . suggest significant and recurrent crisscrossings and linkages between the divorce and a breakdown in the functioning of the caretaking adult, with consequent serious impairment of the parenting capacity. . . . In the case of Alex, the divorce triggered a severe depression which not only seriously interfered with the mother's capacity to parent, but, as suggested, evoked a particular kind of pathogenic ambience which is specifically ominous for the mental health and development of the very young preschool child.[5]

It is not only professionals writing for psychiatric journals who observe "serious impairment of the parenting capacity." It is observed by thousands of fathers who have to watch their children deteriorate progressively and know that legally they can do nothing about it. We asked one father how he handles the situation when his children ask him when they can come and live with him.

5. Wallerstein and Kelly, "The Effects of Parental Divorce," p. 603.

"You stand there," he told us, "and feel your heart being crunched into a thousand pieces."

Tierney's admonition of "Don't cop out!" can have a hollow ring, sometimes.

DROPPING OUT

The most frequent expression for this trend in changing family situations is "runaway wives," which, actually, is quite misleading in this context. The classic example of the runaway wife was Angelina Alioto (wife of San Franciso mayor Joseph Alioto), who disappeared for seventeen days in January 1974. Upon being reunited with her husband, Mrs. Alioto said, "I don't want adulation; all I want is recognition from my husband."

The dropout wife that we are talking about is not, basically, the woman who wants her marriage and family to remain intact but one who wants more recognition of her role within it. We are talking about the woman who is "dropping out" completely from the marriage and responsibility for raising the children. She wants out. We do have to make the distinction here between the "dropout mother" and the woman who has relinquished custody after careful consideration and discussion with her husband, as well as the woman who has lost custody when her husband hired a "bomber" lawyer, and she was reluctant to stage a custody battle for fear of psychic damage to the children, lack of funds, or both. These women deserve more credit than society is often willing to give them.

The responsible mother who relinquishes custody often does so with a realistic, clear-cut concept of what her own postdivorce life will be like as well as with the assurance that her children will thrive well seeing her only occasionally. The media have made much of the dropout wife running off to "do her own thing," leaving her hapless husband to fend for himself as best he can. But many dropout mothers do so more from an inability to cope than from callous heartlessness.

Marilyn, the mother of two girls, seven and two, is herself a product of divorce. Her mother had a series of lovers and resented Marilyn and her younger sister, often screaming and yelling at them. After eight years of split-level boredom, Marilyn took a lover. And another. And another. She found herself screaming at the children constantly. As she told us, "I saw the same pattern repeating itself and felt helpless to stop it. I knew I was destroying the girls. Mike could hire a housekeeper who could give them better care than I ever could."

Cynthia is the mother of three. At first glance, her above-the-knee skirt and long, flowing hair make her look like a post-teen-ager. You don't notice the tiny lines around her eyes until you get up close. Cynthia explains to us that she "married too young." Three babies, one right after the other, robbed her of her young adulthood, she feels. She was caught in a mountain of diapers when the other girls were having fun "at all those demonstrations and things." Lawrence, her husband, working on one Ph.D. after another, was "a grind." Along came Rick, who's "into film," and he's really "with it," Cynthia assures us. She goes back to Lawrence's home one day a week and does some chores for the children, who implore her, along with Lawrence, to come back. But Rick, she tells us, "really makes her feel like a woman." We asked her about her life with Rick.

"Rick really appreciates how I take care of the place and cook for him and everything."

We asked her if she had career plans of her own.

"Oh, I guess I'll go back for my master's some day," she assures us. "Right now I've got a part-time job filing for an insurance company. Rick wants me to pay my own way. He doesn't want me to become dependent. He says it's bad for a woman."

We asked her how Lawrence was managing alone with the children.

"He begs me to come back," she says vaguely.

"And what about the children?" we asked her.

"It's tough sometimes," she tells us. "Especially when Robbie pulls at my skirt when I'm about to leave. I guess it's hard on Robbie," she admits. "After all, he's only two—"

Cynthia's voice trails off. But she perks up as she challenges us: "But I'm entitled to my fun too, you know. I'm young."

Cynthia stands just close enough for us to notice the gray strands in her almost waist-length hair.

Cynthia is keeping the lines of communication open. She has indicated to us that Rick has warned her "against these chicks who get too possessive."

Anna Sklar, in her book, *Runaway Wives,* is actually describing the dropout mother—the woman who leaves her home and children, usually going to a distant state so that communication with her family will remain minimal.

Sometimes, the dropout mother leaves the family home after a series of arguments, with her husband and children imploring her to stay. In other instances, like Chuck's, his wife walked out on three hours' notice.

"What am I going to tell the kids?" he asked her.

"That's your problem," she answered.

In Chuck's case, it was the classic Grade-B movie melodrama. His wife ran off with his business partner. In other cases, it is the promise of a lucrative career for the wife or a "waiting-in-the-wings" lover.

However, most dropout mothers are of the classic, early feminist variety: "I must fulfill myself as a person." These are most of the women described in *Runaway Wives* for whom, often, "fulfillment" takes the form of puttering in clay and/or lesbianism and "getting it together to the point where it's OK to be on welfare."

> "I have a college degree, I'm highly educated, I'm well traveled, I have many advantages, none of which I knew how to use. I'm still not sure . . . of how to use my skills. I'm making them up as I go along," which, she explained, she's been doing for the past twelve years.[6]

Other dropout wives also report making up skills as they go along:

> "I decided to go back to school, but I was really hurting for money. . . . Larry had all these clients," Arlene said, "who wanted a woman they could go out with and feel comfortable with. I would get one hundred dollars for the night."[7]

In commenting on the children, Ms. Sklar continues:

> The only certainty I do have comes from the women and often from the men who were left with the children. Many of the men reported that the children were doing fine and that they, the husbands, had adjusted too. None of the children, as of this writing—and they range from four to sixteen years—had been placed in foster homes or institutions. This fact does not necessarily mean the children did not or will not suffer for their

6. Anna Sklar, *Runaway Wives*, (New York: Coward, McCann & Geoghegan, 1976), p. 31.

7. *Ibid.*, p. 75.

mothers' choice. There are no guarantees, however, that passive acceptance of unhappiness or stunted growth by women will provide a better future for their children.[8]

Most of the custody-fighting fathers we know would regard a dropout mother as a gift dropped out straight from heaven. But there is another side of the coin and, often, after the pottery-puttering life, a dropout mother can get an attack of the "instant madonna" syndrome. She appears properly remorseful and glibly pious in court, and many a custodial father has had his custody status seriously threatened when the bloom begins to fade, or a formerly middle-class mother realizes that custody of her children represents increased welfare payments.

"Husband-dumping" has taken on an aura of chic in some of the more sophisticated quarters of what is loosely known as the "sexual revolution." It can cause problems, however: "One instance of Park Slope husband-dumping was rather dramatic. Thirty-five-year-old Karen, married twelve abrasive years, simply packed her bags one day, leaving her two children, husband and elegant house. . . . Now she makes weekend visits to her children and is trying to figure out what to do when the avowed love of her life takes a challenging position in California and she has to choose between him and her children."[9]

In an article entitled "Runaway Sex," Pat Alison reports on a "de facto Hot Line for runaway wives" she claims to be operating. After citing several "case histories" of wives who left home, hearth, and children in search of "fulfillment," the author offers the following advice to "any husbands out there sneaking a peek at this article to find out what's on their wives' minds":

> . . . there are a lot of husbands out there who are neglecting to slip their spouses the old chocolate bar with sufficient frequency and gusto. The economy's been in a slump—and so have many dicks. A few years ago, women might have put up with this limp state of affairs. . . . But women's lib is letting them look critically at their marriages—not just at who does the dishes, but at the last time they had a good, old-fashioned, rip-roaring fuck.[10]

8. Ibid., pp. 22, 23.
9. Jane Jaffe Young, "Why These Park Slope Women Dumped Their Husbands," *New Woman*, September–October 1975. (Originally printed in *The Village Voice*.)
10. Pat Alison, "Runaway Sex," *New Dawn*, August 1976, p. 87.

The sneaky-peeking husband is further advised:

> She's a lot less likely to head for the bus station if she's got 165 pounds of man pinning her to the mattress. If she's coming, she won't be going.[11]

When a father has custody, most of his problems stem from trying to get his ex to maintain some form of contact with the children. We have not yet reached the stage of equality where a man will fight for custody to hold onto the kids as a means of securing a piece of the wife's income. We have spoken to only one woman who has voluntarily relinquished custody and complains of problems. She has open visitation, the children spend most weekends with her, she has open phone communication, but she feels she is not consulted in medical decisions. She told me she is often tempted to "cop out" because she feels she is up against one of two arguments: "You relinquished custody; you must be a completely cold, unfeeling mother," or "Congratulations! How positively chic of you." She is in the outline stage of a book on "weekend parent," which deals with the trauma of the noncustodial parent from the parent's point of view—not the child's. She feels she is up against societal pressures, not "visitation roulette" on the part of her former husband.

11. Ibid.

10

THE CHILDREN:
IS ANYBODY OUT THERE
LISTENING?

In literature and conversation, when discussing children in relation to divorce, one word inevitably crops up. That word is *pawn*. Of course, *pawn* will be used most frequently when a custody battle ensues, but it is used equally often when custody arrangements are agreed upon and the child is used either to "punish" the ex-spouse or when one parent is trying to become the "favorite." One fact that is rarely or ever mentioned is that children are used as pawns within conventional marriages at least as often as they are in a divorce, and for much the same reasons.

However, the children of divorce are being used as pawns in a much more serious situation than either a court battle or an emotional battle between divorced parents. Specifically, the child of divorce is a pawn among the conflicting armies of experts. These are often not limited to the field of child welfare and/or psychology. They include behaviorists, social workers, champions of divorce, enemies of divorce, religious moderates, religious fanatics, psychiatry moderates, and psychiatry fanatics, not to mention leaders of feminine and feminist movements. They include the man on the street and the woman on the street, who may or may not have M.D.s and/or Ph.D.s, earned legitimately or otherwise. Their viewpoints range from a hand-wringing "The children are doomed" accompanied by appropriate moaning, to "Children are much more resilient than you think" or "The children will just have to learn to adjust" accompanied by an equally appropriate wave of the hand. There are also several thousand gradations in between. Conflicting as they may be on what effect, if any, divorce will have on a child's life, there is one area in which they agree unanimously: the absolute, irrefutable, unassailable righteousness of their particular point of view.

Theories of divorce effect on children reflect theories regarding divorce. Where divorce is regarded as sin or personality failure, "the children are doomed" rationale follows. On the other hand, the "divorce-as-growth" school of thought inevitably carries with it the "children are resilient" slogan. We have yet to encounter theories combining divorce as failure on the part of the spouses but highly beneficial to the children or, conversely, divorce as spiritual salvation to both spouses accompanied by inevitable psychic destruction to the children. The only middle ground we came across emanates from the swinging liberationists. There, the answer to the question about divorce effect on children seems to be, "Who cares?"

The divorce-as-personal-growth theory evolved as part of the "rights" movement, "sexual revolution," and encounter-group-type movements. Prior to that, both established religion and established psychiatry took the same stand regarding divorce, the difference being one of semantics only. What the church called "sin" the psychiatric establishment called "emotional immaturity." Informal research on our part turned up the following startling revelation as to which "experts" advocated divorce as sin/mental illness or mental health: It depended upon whether or not that particular expert had been divorced.

The major "chicken or the egg" question regarding children of divorce and subsequent problems relating to emotional disorder and/or juvenile delinquency discloses two major discoveries; namely, (1) divorce and socioemotional problems are directly related, and (2) divorce and socioemotional problems are totally unrelated. For every researcher providing data correlating divorce and juvenile delinquency, there are at least three providing equally impressive data proving that (1) there is no correlation between divorce and juvenile delinquency, and (2) there is at least as much juvenile delinquency and related problems from children of two-parent homes as from children of divorce. As a result, we are not concentrating on quotes from conflicting experts. Instead, we have chosen to delve into the factors that the experts have chosen to overlook; namely, which circumstances surrounding which divorces have produced which detrimental effects in which (if any) children?

Most divorce research is based on problem children, and efforts have been made to correlate the disturbances with the divorce. Needless to say, findings showed that most of the children's problems had their origins in the strife- and tension-ridden environments inevitably generated in strife- and tension-ridden marriages. To our knowledge no one has ever taken a random group of adults who are functioning efficiently in job, family, and community, and attempted to find out what percentage of them came from intact or broken homes and the quality of those homes. If such research were ever undertaken, it could well turn up data to the effect that many children who had tearfully cried, "But I wish my Mommy and Daddy could stay together," have grown up into adults with a deeper degree of understanding and human sensitivity than those whose childhood was relatively trauma-free.

More unfortunately, no long-range research has been undertaken on successfully adjusted divorce children, following them through adulthood, to determine which factors preceding, during, and following the divorce contributed to that successful adjustment. We have no statistics available on how many tension-ridden two-parent homes miraculously become transformed into tension-free one-parent homes, although the aggressively prodivorce faction would have us believe that this is an inevitable result.

Needless to say, if a child's postdivorce life is characterized by a tension-free environment and his or her predivorce life was a constant round of bickering, arguing, or worse—ominous, clenched-teeth silence—he or she can certainly be said to have benefited from the divorce, although the divorce process itself may have been traumatic.

Until very recently, the one-parent home referred to the mother-only home. We have no way of knowing how many of these mother-headed homes provided for meaningful father–child interaction following divorce, assuming that (1) the father was living, and (2) he was eager to maintain a relationship with the children. In other words, with the mountains of research available on divorce effect on children, we have no more information on *quality of divorce* than we have on quality of marriage. We do know, however, that the divorce process is traumatic for children, whether their reaction is one of hysterical temper tantrums or, more dangerously, withdrawn silence, known in the vernacular as "keeping cool." Tragically, it is this latter reaction that gives divorcing parents the soothing illusion that their child has escaped danger.

What usually happens is that the children are caught between these two philosophies of doom and blithe denial from those around them. Grandparents will usually heap the doom upon them while their parents expend all their energy in studiously avoiding their cries (albeit silent) for help. One thing these two philosophies have in common: They are equally destructive to the child. Therefore, the child who becomes the pawn of these conflicting concepts can be compared to a person with a broken ankle caught between two philosophies: one declaring that he or she is destined to be a cripple all his or her life, and the other denying that anything was wrong in the first place. The effect is the same in both instances: Constructive or corrective action will not be taken.

No aspect of divorce effect on children is studied more thoroughly than breaking the news to a child that a divorce is forthcoming. Here again, there is no dearth of philosophy. At one extreme we have this approach: "We may as well begin by admitting frankly that we really cannot explain divorce to children. The best we can hope to do is to help them come to terms with those consequences of divorce that affect them personally."[1]

At the other extreme we have the "swinging divorce" concept, reinforced by schools of thought that marriage gone sour can only be detrimental to both spouses as well as to the children, and the best thing that each spouse can do is get out of it—fast. It is these children who are most prone to the "Mumzy and Dadzy are getting this little divorcey-poo and even though we don't love each other any more we still love you" syndrome. And for those parents who have been made aware that divorce is inevitably accompanied by guilt in children, there's always the comforting "It isn't your fault. Daddy isn't going away because you were bad" as an afterthought.

A third grade schoolteacher we know reported the following incident to us: An eight-year-old girl in her class came to school one day completely withdrawn and silent. Being one of those teachers with a heightened awareness of responsibility for all aspects of a child's development, she called the child aside after class and asked what was troubling her. After the usual "Oh, nothing," the child admitted that on the previous night her parents had announced that they were about to be divorced. The teacher tried to be as comforting as she could and pointed out that many children in the class also had

1. John L. Thomas, "A Priest's Views on Children of Divorce," *Explaining Divorce to Children*, ed. Earle A. Grollman (Boston: Beacon Press, 1969), p. 179.

parents who were divorced. The child replied, "But you don't understand. They were *smiling*. They just sat there and *smiled.*"

Fortunately, we are on the threshold of a breakthrough in obtaining meaningful data on the long-term effects of divorce on children. For this breakthrough, we have two remarkable and sensitive researchers at the University of California and the Marin County Community Health Center—Judith S. Wallerstein and Joan B. Kelly to thank. Their findings have been published extensively in professional journals and are scheduled to appear in book form shortly. Hailed as a landmark in research on the subject, the Children of Divorce Project was started in 1971 and Wallerstein and Kelly are currently analyzing the results of four years of intensive follow-up. Admittedly, Marin County is a middle-class suburb of San Francisco and has one of the highest divorce rates in the country.

These two researchers have reason to look somewhat askance at the "Mumzy and Dadzy and this little divorcey-poo" rationale:

> A whole range of symptoms and behaviors, some of them alarming, appeared in many of the preschoolers almost immediately following the family breakup, and the researchers were shocked to discover how few parents failed to connect the troubling new behaviors with the divorce. . . . The seven- and eight-year-olds seemed to have few ways available to deal with sorrow. More than half the children in this age group changed their behavior at school . . . divorce froze them and their academic achievement plummeted.[2]

It should be pointed out that the children of this project were reported as having been progressing normally in family, school, and friendship interaction at the time of divorce. While the glib evasiveness faction will hasten to assure anyone that yes, indeedy, there may be problems at the beginning, but "the children will adjust," we learn otherwise:

> Other youngsters seemed to weather the separation of the parents with remarkable ease, only to have a delayed reaction. Eight-year-old Philip, for example, showed no change in his behavior for the six months following the separation. . . . Then one

2. Shirley Streshinsky, "How Divorce Really Affects Children: A Major Report, *Redbook*, September 1976, p. 132.

day he refused to take off his jacket at school, and for the next three months he was withdrawn and depressed. He neglected his schoolwork, refused to play with the other children on the block, and dropped out of the club he had helped organize only a few weeks before.[3]

Fortunately, Philip's problems were of short duration:

Just as suddenly he rallied, picked up where he had left off and seemed his old self. In some way the researchers didn't totally understand, Philip seemed to have come to terms with his pain.[4]

One of the most promising trends in helping children deal with divorce comes from those who are not trying to take the denial route in evaluating divorce effect on children. The Evergreen Developmental Center, a private community social service center in a suburb of Denver, has set up a program called Children Facing Divorce, providing a group setting for children to deal with their feelings. Here again, it is made startlingly clear that the chin-up pose assumed by so many children can mask deep, underlying disturbance:

Most [children] were coping with the situation stoically. Oh, their grades in school had taken the usual nose dive. Some were having trouble sleeping. Grumpiness, daydreaming, and temper tantrums were on the upswing. But for the most part these children were adjusting. It was their parents (at least the ones with custody) who had assumed, accurately, that divorce must be as traumatic for children as it is for adults.[5]

The Evergreen Developmental Center offers a highly sophisticated program for the children, including videotape. Here again, the children are encouraged to talk about their feelings and share them with one another. Another aspect of the guilt experienced by children is not so much their negative feelings toward the custodial or noncustodial parent or, perhaps, both, but for the positive feelings toward the absent parent. Quoting Dr. Gordon Farley, acting director of the Department of Child Psychiatry at the University of Colorado Medi-

3. Ibid., p. 134.
4. Ibid., p. 134.
5. Elizabeth Jean Pasco, "Helping Children Survive Divorce," *Woman's Day*, August 1976, p. 2.

cal Center: "It may be asking too much for an angry parent to sing the praises of the other. But a child does need some kind of permission to love his absent parent. . . . Children are in a loyalty bind. They feel they're wronging one parent if they like the one who has gone away. They need to know it's OK."[6]

Wallerstein and Kelly point out that one of the major factors in helping children cope with divorce is flexibility in visitation arrangements: "The only children satisfied with the visiting situation were those who were able to see their father several times a week. Others felt deprived; they said that seeing the missing parent twice a month was not enough."[7]

For a long time, one of the clichés dear to the hearts (and mouths) of the glib denial, prodivorce faction was that father absence was not to be taken seriously as long as the child's material needs were met, thereby contributing to the "roll over, play dead, pay up" concept of the model divorced father. Where father absence is concerned, many people will point out (backed up by impressive research) that children brought up by widowed mothers have displayed an outstanding ability to cope with the situation and often have made a far above average adult life adjustment. As the quality of divorce is rarely taken into consideration in drawing conclusions about divorce effect on children, so has the quality of father absence been grossly neglected in evaluating the effect of a mother-only or mother-predominant home on children. This oversight has been scrutinized thoroughly in a report from the Office of Child Development of HEW. Although it is entitled "Boys in Fatherless Families," many of the findings apply to girls as well.

> There has been repeated evidence that when factors within the home were studied, family climate has been a more potent variable than father absence per se; that socioeconomic situation has overshadowed father absence; that the mother's response to the father's absence is a crucial factor, mediating the impact of that absence on a child; that the mother's definition of the father's absence and of her role in the current situation affect her treatment of the child; and that the child's individual characteristics affect both her treatment and his response. It

6. Ibid., pp. 4, 98.
7. Streshinsky, "How Divorce Really Affects Children," p. 136.

must be assumed that the individual characteristics of the mother, including her ability to cope with her current situation, are crucial factors in her response; and that all of these are affected by the social and economic circumstances of the family, as well as by community norms and attitudes.[8]

Much of the foregoing could lead us to believe that current court practices of custody and visitation (the latter not always enforced) could create a situation where a child becomes a victim not only of impaired father interaction but of the fear of expressing positive feelings regarding the father, compounded by impaired functioning in the parent role on the part of the custodial mother.

At least at the middle-class, upper-educated level, many divorced parents will make an attempt to provide whatever professional help they feel is necessary in their children's life adjustment, and the more expensive the better. Too often, psychotherapy is hailed as the panacea for the emotional problems of children as well as adults. Ralph Ober, former president of Parents Without Partners, cautions against automatic psychotherapy: "Children often pay a high price for psychotherapy. The risk is always there that one might establish a lifelong pattern of dependency and poor self-confidence as a result of ill-advised action."[9]

Psychotherapy-oriented parents can easily fall into the trap of "playing doctor" with their children in a misguided attempt to help children talk about their problems. This is made clear in *Part-Time Father,* under the heading, "You Are Not His Therapist":

> Trying to understand your child's behavior does not mean trying to "treat" him. You are the child's father, not his therapist. You are blessed and burdened with all the privileges and responsibilities of fatherhood. To talk things over with the adolescent, each hearing the other out, can help to clear the air when disagreements get out of hand. It can even strengthen the relationship. But telling him *why* he is behaving badly can only confuse and upset him.[10]

8. Elizabeth Herzog and Cecilia E. Sudia, "Boys in Fatherless Families," DHEW Publication No. (OCD) 72–73, 1971, p. 85.

9. Ralph Ober, "Parents Without Partners—with Children of Divorce," *Explaining Divorce to Children,* ed. Earl A. Grellman (Boston: Beacon Press, 1969), p. 149.

10. Edith Atkin and Estelle Rubin, *Part-Time Father* (New York: Vanguard Press, 1976), p. 186.

One of the potential problems facing a child of divorce is the fear of being "different" from his friends. Of course, this will be exaggerated in families and communities where divorce is relatively infrequent. Parents Without Partners (see chapter 12) feels that one of its most beneficial services to children is the sense of community created for children of divorce. Rap groups are springing up where children can air their feelings regarding divorce in a nonthreatening environment. Sharing of anxieties in a peer-group climate has proven more beneficial to many children (as well as adults) than the traditional psychologist–patient relationship, where children have been intimidated by the "cross-examination" ambience created by professionals. Not all leaders of these rap groups are professionally trained, but they do have the proverbial "way with children." Privately or community sponsored, they are often available at costs that are not prohibitive. SOLO is a single-parents' group sponsored by the Mental Health Association of Oregon, providing services for parents as well as children. The following is from their newspaper:

HAVING A SINGLE PERSON AS A PARENT

A group for young people, ages eight through twelve, who live with (or visit) single parents. To discuss: how they feel about divorce; the absent parent; parent's dating; responsibilities, etc., with empathetic big sister/big brother type adults. Leaders are Paul and Linda, who have a special way with kids, though not professionally trained. $1.00 1st child, $2.00 maximum.[11]

It is a generally accepted theorem that a strife-ridden two-parent environment creates more long-range problems than a harmonious one-parent environment. We cannot point the finger of guilt at parents who divorce. Nor can we propose that children will inevitably undergo psychic pain as a result of that divorce.

But when that pain is trivialized or ignored completely, the finger of guilt might well be pointed at some of the smug clichés that we, parents and nonparents alike, use in an attempt to justify our nonguilt.

Is anybody out there listening?

11. *Solo Center News* (Portland, Oreg.), October 1976, p.3.

11
KIDNAP!

Dear Ms. Winkler:

I am perfectly willing to cooperate with any media of any kind. . . . However, there is NO GODDAM WAY you or any other reporter is going to interview the operating section of the underground. I'm not about to compromise security for some of these men—they'd be dead in a week if somebody found out they're connected with me. Only C _____ and M _____ are in a position for an interview. If you want either of them, it works like this: Contact J _____ who will arrange for a personal interview with M _____ and his two children. M _____ will be brought in through a quite elaborate security system for the interview, then returned. You will not be allowed to use your own auto, for fear of radio tracers, and your equipment will be searched, *as will your person,* for radio mikes. You may possibly be blindfolded to prevent you from revealing where the interview takes place—that is up to J _____.

For C _____ I can arrange the interview *under much more strict security.* . . . [italics ours]

Although neither Ira nor Win was about to undergo any inadvertent proctological examination in the name of investigative reporting, we couldn't help but wonder what the writer had in mind when he referred to "much more strict security." The letter was written by one of the more flamboyant leaders of the "child-snatching" movement, and his "perfect willingness to cooperate with any media of any kind" has proven to be something of a nuisance to more than one reporter and TV newscaster.

Technically and legally, the word *kidnap* cannot be used when it involves a parent taking his or her own child. The expression "child-snatching," however, is gaining in popularity. Whatever you want to call it, child-snatching resulted in 100,000 cases in 1975 by either private detective agencies or individuals working on an expense-plus-contribution basis, although "informal" child-retrieval figures—children being taken by relatives and friends of parents— are estimated at closer to 200,000. Not every "child-retrieval" incident involves the gangbusters-type melodrama indicated in the opening letter of this chapter. As we pointed out earlier, a child planting himself at the doorstep of the noncustodial father can leave him open to charges of illegal possession of the child, known more often as custodial interference. How many cases like that of Ken, whose son, Brian, was "taken for a ride" by his mother, go unreported each year can only be guessed at. Whatever the colloquialism, whatever the reason, the idea of any parent, with or without a custody decree in hand, snatching a child at play from the home of the other parent can only provoke reactions of horrified disgust from most of us. It is repugnant, and if we hear of any parent resorting to these techniques, our reaction will be almost universal: Leave the child with whichever parent he has been; the situation will only be worsened by the snatching experience.

For purposes of clarification, we will divide child-snatching into two categories: *child-grabbing,* where the noncustodial parent or the parent who fears that he or she will not be awarded custody consequently disappears with the child to regions unknown; and *child-retrieval,* where the parent, usually custodial or custodial-confident, takes back the child from the parent who has absconded with him or her in the first place. Lines between legal and illegal, moral and immoral, become increasingly blurred where child-snatching is concerned. The trend of increased custody awards to fathers has resulted in an increase of mothers who abscond, although child-snatchers and detectives we have spoken to tell us that their clients are split about evenly between mothers and fathers. It should be pointed out that the "professional" child-snatchers—either private investigators or individuals who have made this their specialty— operate legally to the degree that the parent must have a custody decree in his or her hand before he or she will be accepted as a client.

Gene Austin of Foley, Missouri, is one of the better-known names among child-snatchers who operate legally. His fee, usually $300 plus expenses, make his services far less expensive than those of licensed private investigators.

Bill Ralston, director of United Parents of Absconded Children also works on a basis of expenses plus contribution from his clients. Ralston is the father whose wife absconded with the children three years ago when he was awarded custody and who, as of this writing, has not yet retrieved the children.

The rise in the incidence of child-snatching, whether it be abduction or retrieval, is one of the loose ends left dangling by the adoption of no-fault divorce laws. The major headache is that child-snatching is not against any federal law if a parent is the snatcher. The FBI has consistently opposed bills that would involve them in finding abducted children. The only hope, at this point, is that uniform child-custody laws will be enacted and there can be federal intervention when parents abscond with their children. The most publicized case of parental child-snatching involved Seward Prosser Mellon in March 1975.

Mellon received custody of his two daughters in Pittsburgh in April 1974. In December of 1975 he sent the two girls for a visit with their mother in North Carolina, with the understanding that they would be returned by Christmas. His former wife took the two children to New York, where she obtained a custody decree. Mellon appealed to the Justice Department in Washington to get his children back legally and was told that his was a "civil, domestic matter." Mellon said he would take "whatever steps were necessary" to get the children back. He hired three men to snatch the children, in spite of the bodyguard their mother had hired, and got them back to Pennsylvania in a series of cars and private planes.

Mellon had custody of his two children in Pennsylvania, while his wife had custody in New York. It is difficult in such circumstances to comment on which parent is taking the law into his or her own hands. Each parent is legally "in the right."

It is this lack of legal recourse that is accounting for the rise in child-snatching. Earlier in this book, Ralston described his dismay upon learning that while the court was willing to award him custody of his children, it was not available for enforcing the ruling. Since his wife had absconded with the children some time before, he at last concluded, "My custody order seemingly is not worth the paper it is written on." Ralston tells us here about the subsequent founding of United Parents of Absconded Children:

Initially, I . . . felt I was the only parent walking the face of this earth experiencing this horrible injustice and terribly frustrating hell. I felt hopelessly alone, as most victimized parents typically do. However, as time passed and I learned of similar parents, I realized that I was not alone and that all cases had the same horrifying characteristics. There are several common denominators among all other cases I have investigated—no effective legal recourse, very little and in most cases no assistance from our courts and authorities in locating and returning our absconded children, even to the point of encouraging, facilitating and protecting absconding parents; victimized parents forced to spend exorbitant amounts of money (without the wealth of a Seward Prosser Mellon) attempting to locate their stolen children and to enforce their judicial custody-visitation orders, when this should be enforced through our legal and law enforcement processes. I became very much appalled by the blatant injustice suffered by these many victimized parents and the ineffectiveness and apathy of our system and, most importantly, the unstable life of limbo thrust upon our young children. Somebody had to do something.

When we talked with Ralston, he pointed out one aspect of child-snatching that is usually overlooked in the whole concept—the physical danger involved to the child, the retrieving parent, and the driver. There is one case on record in which both a father and his child were killed when the getaway car was forced off the road. Both Ralston and Austin, who sometimes work together on cases, feel that the safety factor is one of the most important components of their operation. They often have several cars and drivers waiting at close intervals to avoid breakneck speed, which is usually involved in getaways. Another aspect of both Ralston's and Austin's operations is that they both insist that the parent be present during the retrieval. This, they each explain, is to minimize trauma to the child, the existence of which they are not trying to deny. According to Austin, the child's initial shock at being snatched abates as soon as he or she recognizes the parent.

The three men kept changing rented cars. One had dyed his hair so he wouldn't be so easily recognized.

Their mission: snatch a ten-year-old boy and his eight-year-old brother and get them across the state line. . . . On the fifth day, they finally got a clear shot at the children. . . . The ten-year-old had a running start on his bicycle and had to be knocked off it. . . . The eight-year-old was snapped up easily. Both were tossed into the strange car.

The children were terrified—until they recognized the man with the dyed hair. He was their father, Arlie Wayne Haskins.[1]

We spoke to both Haskins and his older son, Eric. Haskins, a thirty-seven-year-old nuclear chemist, is neither a wild man nor a vindictive one. He had won custody of the boys in Alabama; his former wife had won custody in Massachusetts. He had tried to get his custody rights recognized in Massachusetts, but Federal Judge W. Arthur Garrity, Jr., in Boston refused to hear his case, as did the Supreme Court.

We were more concerned about the children's postsnatching adjustment than the gangbusters-type logistics of the snatch itself. Haskins explained to us that the boys are "back home," doing well in school, and all three of them are living with Haskins's family pending completion of their new house. He did point out, however, that the fear of a repeat performance on the part of the boys' mother is a realistic fear, and he has enlisted the cooperation of both school officials and neighbors in "keeping an eye on them" when they're out playing. Eric, the older boy, sounded to us as though he's enjoying the "neighborhood hero" role immensely and told us that although, at first, both he and his younger brother were worried about a counter-snatching, they both now feel that "everybody is watching out for us." Haskins told us that he encourages frequent telephone contact between the boys and their mother.

We asked both Austin and Ralston about their clients and what similarities, if any, were to be found among their cases. Austin pointed out to us that his clients run the gamut from farmers to doctors but did add, "They've got to be able to afford our fees." He mentioned that those who could not afford the usual $1,000 in expenses plus the $300 fee would probably attempt to do the job themselves, in which case the accident risk is so much higher. He also mentioned that for those where money was no object, expensive private investigators would probably be used, especially inasmuch as these agencies did not insist that the client actually take part in the

1. Kay Bartlett, "Youngsters the Pawns in Custody Snatchings," (AP), *World-Herald* (Omaha, Neb.), 19 September, 1976.

physical snatching. Both Austin and Ralston specialize in retrievals rather than abduction, especially since they insist that their clients have the custody decree.

Both Austin and Ralston reported one strikingly similar characteristic of all snatchings: A child is usually *absconded with* from a middle-class environment to a slum situation and *retrieved* back into the middle-class environment. That was the situation in Haskins's case; his children were living on welfare, although his wife was employed as a professional. Austin and Ralston are fighting for legislation to recognize and cope with the problem.

Both Ralston and Austin have made one statement that has been corroborated by quite a few fathers we have spoken to: Their lawyers have advised them to "grab the kids and run." It is difficult for us to comment on the morality or immorality of child-snatching. The question that comes to our minds is: "Snatched from what to what? From whom to whom?

Screeching cars, dyed hair, and other "get-'em Charlie" tactics in child-snatching represent only the tip of the iceberg in custody cases. A divorced fathers' group in Canada distributes the following information:

WHY FATHERS ARE ABDUCTING THEIR CHILDREN

If the judicial system in Ontario cannot act more expeditiously and with some concern for the rights of the children and the fathers, then abduction by the father is going to become a common event.

More lawyers are thusly advising fathers to take such action after the mother has disappeared with the furniture and the children.

During a TV interview with a representative from the Society recently the hostess asserted that fathers should have every right to walk out with the children and desert, just as mothers have been doing.

Imagine the ordeal of children and the father who might be separated for one, two or three years before custody is decided. Why should they be deprived of one another for this period of time. Why should a mother be allowed to "walk out" without fear of reprisal from the judicial system or from society? What about the children who might not want to be living with their mother?

> If the judicial system cannot radically improve its concern and priorities for placement of the children, then we give our full blessings to those fathers who act in good conscience.[2]

Not every child is retrieved from an absconding parent. Court practice of placing a child of a proven unfit mother in an institution or foster home rather than awarding custody to the father is becoming more and more commonplace. We received a series of phone calls from a man named Vito, who had gotten our names from a social worker.

Vito called Ira and told him he had kidnapped his own son. He promised to stay in touch with us but told us that he had no phone number he could leave. He sketched the story to us briefly in a series of phone calls. Two years ago he had lost a custody fight for his son, then aged eight. When his former wife had to be institutionalized for child abuse, Vito took the child into his home. The police broke into Vito's home, drugged the boy, and put him into a child detention home in New York City which has earned itself the reputation of "Alcatraz, Junior." Vito snatched the boy from the home. He did not give us any details but promised to meet with us at a later date "when things cooled down." At that point he left us a phone number. We asked how his son was doing after the experience.

"He doesn't like living like a fugitive," Vito told us, "but he knows that things are going to settle down soon and that he's going to live with me."

We tried to contact Vito when we hoped things had "cooled down," but his phone had been disconnected.

Stuart did not employ the services of an Austin or a Ralston to get Jonathan, now six, back from his former wife and her second husband. He had no trouble gaining custody when Jonathan was eighteen months old. His former wife had moved into a hippie crash pad and soon realized that the baby cramped her style somewhat. However, when she made the transition from crash pad to split-level suburbia, replete with crew-cutted husband and a new baby, she suddenly developed a strong maternal instinct toward Jonathan. Not wanting to keep him from knowing his half sister, Stuart agreed to let Jonathan spend a year with his mother and her new family. He

---

2. *News Media Information*, Society of Single Fathers, Willowdale, Ontario, July 1975.

became perturbed when, as he puts it, "they were trying to make a Jesus freak out of Jonathan."

It was agreed that Jonathan was to be returned to Stuart at the end of June. Jonathan was not on the plane that Stuart went to meet. He telephoned his former wife, who began stalling. Her husband got on the phone and tried to persuade Stuart to leave Jonathan with them, "so the boy can get a good, Christian upbringing."

"I guess I kind of freaked out," Stuart explains. "I got this friend of mine and told him we were going to California. Fast."

Stuart and his friend set up a network based roughly on the Austin–Ralston system. They took Jonathan from a schoolyard, whisked him to the home of friends, and took a bus out of California at 5:00 A.M. to Wyoming to catch a plane for New York.

"The paranoia is still with me," Stuart tells us. "We spent four days looking over our shoulders."

He assures us that he had the custody decree in his pocket throughout the entire incident.

Most parental "kidnapping" cases are largely unreported when the children are called "runaways"—they simply run away from the custodial mother to the father's home. As we reported earlier, one lawyer termed this phenomenon an "informal custody arrangement." As we also reported, on more occasions the father is ordered to return the children promptly and the children can be threatened with institutionalization. As the police are often called, the children run the further risk of a juvenile delinquency record. These children, at least, have the consolation that they are wanted by their fathers and can look forward to the day when they are no longer declared minors. Not all children are that lucky. We heard a story about one father who was *not* in our sampling.

Marlene, aged thirty-four, realized that her marriage to Harry had reached the state where a divorce would have been the best decision all around, especially for the two children, Kevin, thirteen, and Donna, nine. There was never any custody fight. Harry had a woman waiting in the wings. Although Donna adjusted fairly well, Kevin began displaying serious adjustment symptoms, including truancy and petty larceny. Marlene, an attractive, college-educated woman, went the whole route where Kevin was conerned—school psychologists, private psychotherapy, trying to get her brothers to spend more time with Kevin, after-school activities in the affluent community where they lived. But Kevin wasn't having any. On numerous occasions he ran away to the apartment his father shared with his girlfriend and was turned out by both of them. Harry, who was meticulous about keeping up custody payments and took the two children to a movie every other Sunday, fulfilled the legal criteria of a responsible divorced father. Shortly after Harry and his girlfriend moved to Florida, Kevin was apprehended, trying to hold up a small store. He wanted the money to go to his father.

Still, the ingrained prejudice that children are the exclusive property of the biological mother has a stranglehold on all of us. We don't want to give it up. We tend to make excuses for a mother whose maternal instinct has gone awry. The father who takes his children away from their mother, no matter what the justification, is regarded not only as performing an unnatural act but breaking the law as well.

Jake "kidnapped" his three children three times during his fifteen-month custody battle.

"It's tough enough taking three kids," he tells us, "but when you have to start kidnapping clothes, bicycles, books, and a couple of hamsters, you need a couple of station wagons."

We couldn't help asking him, "How could you take the law into your own hands?"

Slowly, patiently, Jake began to describe the children's insistence that they live with him, his former wife's drinking, the succession of men staying over, the shambles the house had become.

"Very easily," he assures us.

12

HELP FOR THE DIVORCED FATHER— AND HIS CHILDREN

The popular image of the divorced father is the same as the image of the divorced man in general—carefree, gay blade, charmer, ladies' man, and most emphatically, the major asset to a dinner party. In contrast is the image of the divorced or otherwise "unattached woman"—a liability to the dinner party by virtue of being a threat to married women and a reputed easy conquest for their husbands.

A recent article states: "In the land of the dinner party, the extra man is king . . . the dinner party is ubiquitous. Women who are unmarried and otherwise unattached are ubiquitous, too."[1]

The article goes on to describe the eligibility scale of the extra man. Diplomats, oil men, doctors, widowers, and divorced men (employment status not specified) are preferred, in descending order. Homosexuals will do in a pinch, "as long as they don't try to dominate the evening." The tales of sexual prowess attributed to the divorced man (primarily by the still-married man) would make the career of a prize bull seem pale in comparison. Divorce is glamorized and romanticized in the men's service magazines (*Playboy,* etc.), as is marriage in the women's service magazines.

The divorced man as combination satyr and Casanova might have some reality among men earning $150,000 a year and over or gigolos looking for women with independent incomes of $150,000 a year and over, but for the divorced father in the $20,000-and-under bracket, the closest he gets to the *Playboy* life-style is often a subscription to

1. John Corry, "The Ever-Popular Extra Man Who Comes to Dinner," *New York Times,* 22 November, 1976, p. C-17.

one of the skin magazines, glanced through at a room at the YMCA if he has to pay alimony in addition to child support.

We all have heard and read about the plight of the divorced mother whose support payments and, often, alimony cannot possibly begin to cover expenses. We have found out one thing in our research regarding settlements and child support: It is never enough according to the woman; it is always too much according to the man. A woman accustomed to living at the $60,000-a-year level during her marriage will cry poverty when she is expected to live and raise her children on $30,000 per year. A divorced father we heard about whose annual income is $150,000 is living on $15,000 per year and claims he can't make ends meet. A great deal has been said about the divorced mother whose life-style undergoes "downward social mobility" although she keeps the family home. Not as much has been said about the divorced father living in a one-room apartment in order to keep up the home he once called his. Much has been said about the emotional attachment of a woman to her home; in fact, supposedly the "nesting instinct" is secondary only to the maternal instinct in the priorities of a woman. Less has been said about a man's attachment to his home and its meaning to him. A man may lose his major sense of accomplishment, his hobbies, his workshop, and his status as host as the result of divorce. Outside of the elegant dinner party set, the man who was accustomed to carving at his own table can begin to feel like a charity case when he's always on the receiving end of the dinner invitation. If his wife had someone waiting in the wings prior to the divorce, he feels laughed at behind his back by the insensitive and pitied condescendingly by his friends. He will have the label of "bastard" placed on him in direct proportion to his former wife's inability to cope with her divorce status. If his former wife "falls apart" throughout and following the divorce and her ability to cope with household and child care deteriorates as a result, she will receive sympathy from friends and family. If he should "fall apart," he is still expected to perform to standard on an often demanding job, especially in a tight employment market. He is required to pay for the services of a lawyer whose high fees are in direct proportion to his skill at vilifying the father. He is neither encouraged nor expected to "cry on anyone's shoulder." Most courses and lectures given by civic groups and single-parent organizations are slanted toward the problems of divorced women.

Joseph Epstein's book, *Divorced in America*, is one that we can recommend highly. It describes not only the financial and emotional limbo of so many divorced men but the plight of the involved father as well. The proponents of divorce as a casual inconvenience but a necessary step in personal growth not only trivialize the effect of divorce on children but also consider the emotional ties of a father as being beside the point.

The divorced father has to face the fact that if his emotional ties to his children are strong, those ties can be the most potent weapon his former wife can and will use against him, especially if she is disappointed in her postdivorce adjustment. We have seen too many cases where relations between divorced parents have been civil until the husband enters into a relationship with a woman on a more-than-casual basis.

Fortunately, we are on the threshold of enlightened recognition of problems facing divorced fathers and constructive options are available to men in coping with all aspects of their postdivorce life, including relationships with the children. In the following sections, we are outlining services that will be detailed in the appendixes and, wherever possible, describing reactions of fathers who have participated in them. We hasten to point out, however, that reactions to these services vary; while many men may have benefited from group experiences ranging from emotional reaction to the divorce to parent-children activities, others have found them inadequate to their needs. It should also be pointed out that certain organizations have different appeal to different people and, also, the character of chapters of specific organizations can vary from one community to another. We would also like to point out that many organizations listed offer multifaceted services for both parents and children; consequently, there may be some duplication. Many people have found specific services offered by multiservice organizations helpful to them and/or their children but tend to back off from them as "package deals." We do hope, however, that our readers will look into what is available and give themselves and their children fair chances.

LEGAL

This is an area where past history appears bleakest but the future seems most hopeful. More progress has been made in a father's chance for obtaining custody over the past two years than over the past fifty. As this book is being written, change is taking place not only in courtrooms but in the minds and hearts of fathers who will no longer tolerate the second-class-parent role.

Most divorced fathers, especially those who have been through a custody battle, have a hatred of lawyers bordering on the pathological or the realistic, depending upon your point of view and their experience. Unfortunately, the word *lawyer* is synonymous with *bomber* or *bumbler* (or both) to them, and many of them have had a series of bitter and costly experiences with a series of costly lawyers. Every divorced father we've spoken to sings virtually the same refrain: "If only I knew about lawyers at the beginning of the divorce what I know now." Most of them evaluate their choice of lawyers the way they evaluate their choice of wives. "Naïve" and "innocent" is how they describe themselves.

The major error these men made, they feel, was in their choice of a lawyer when the divorce was being contemplated. Because of lack of experience combined with the emotional turmoil they were undergoing, most men applied the following criteria to their choice of lawyers: "Sam has been doing the family's legal work for years" and "My neighbor plays golf with this lawyer and says he's really one hell of a terrific guy."

However, the major problem we have encountered among the fathers we have spoken to is that *none of them considered fighting for custody when the divorce was contemplated.* Most divorces started out as no-fault, with complete agreement between the spouses at the outset. The two prime motivating factors for a father fighting for custody are (1) visitation roulette or visitation denial on the part of the custodial mother, and (2) the emotional and psychological deterioration of the custodial mother and her consequent inability to provide adequate care for the children. Another instance we hear of frequently is the father who was refused custody at the time of divorce because he was unable to "provide an adequate home" (as a result of being ordered to support the "adequate home" of his former wife) and may have subsequently remarried a woman who can make a financial contribution to the household.

Speaking to both fathers and lawyers (and sometimes combinations of the two), we heard the same advice repeated constantly: "Find out the lawyer's stand on father custody before engaging his or her services." The usual guideline in choosing a lawyer for a divorce is to request a list of specialists in matrimonial law from the American Bar Association. We must point out that the father-custody or joint-custody specialist is a very recent innovation, and as we have observed in previous chapters, many family law specialists are still shocked and horrified at the idea of fathers having custody.

While Appendix C details the services of a few legal advice referral associations, it should be pointed out that the services of these organizations are not limited to their geographic areas. The lawyers they recommend do consult with out-of-state lawyers. Virtually all organized divorced fathers' groups offer advice on fighting *pro se,* but most of them limit their membership within their states.

EVALUATION PANELS

This is a fairly recent development leading to the creation of the National Organization to Insure Support Enforcement (NOISE) and the Custody Study Institute of America (see Appendix B) and would probably come under the heading of children's rights. Basically, their aims are to create an evaluation panel consisting of psychologists, social workers, doctors, lawyers, and sometimes educators to determine the best interests of the child in a specific case rather than leave everything to the judge. Their function is to make recommendations to the courts based on their findings. Their services are nationwide, and literature is available upon request.

DIVORCED FATHERS' GROUPS

While these groups are known for their legal and paralegal advice, it is generally agreed that the group support the members give one another is their greatest benefit. Most of them limit their services to members of their states. Appendix A lists what we consider to be the most rational and responsible ones. We do not claim this to be a complete listing. We have chosen to eliminate those that stress law-breaking, fanaticism, and pathological woman-hating. Some of those listed have publications of interest to out-of-staters, and these are noted. Most of them are eager to cooperate and share findings with other groups. They also give advice on how to start similar groups in other states. Some of them, in addition to legal and paralegal advice, offer supportive services such as rap groups, finding housing for the newly divorced or newly custodial father, as well as helping him organize his household for child care. Some have strong media connections.

RAP AND DISCUSSION GROUPS

Most single-parent organizations offer this as part of their total service picture, most notably, Parents Without Partners. Single-parent and child-help groups are listed in Appendix B. Many men, at least initially, prefer an all-men's group. Divorced fathers' groups provide these on either an informal or an organized basis. In addition to the single-parents' organizations, there are also groups for divorced people, most of which have a high parent membership. We are listing some here which, we believe, have special merit. Some of them have chapters nationwide; others are local but welcome inquiries on how to get similar groups started. Although their results can be therapeutic, they are not to be considered therapy groups. Some of them are led by trained leaders; others are not. They do stress the group support concept rather than the authoritarian expert–patient relationship. They stress the emotional rather than the legal or financial side of divorce. In addition, many of them are low-cost, request a modest contribution, or, if supported by the community, are free. Complete details on contacting these organizations can be found in Appendix B.

North American Conference of Separated and Divorced Catholics
Boston, Massachusetts

The non-Catholic as well as the Catholic would do well to look into their services. Their publications offer sensitive, understanding insight into all divorce-related problems, in addition to those relevant to Catholicism. They also sponsor an excellent newsletter, *Divorce*, subscription, $7.00 per year. We were impressed by the variety and caliber of their leaflets, ranging in price from $.10 to $.50. We would especially recommend "Guidelines for Self-Help Rap Groups," by Carolyn Jenks, Order No. 220, $.20. Completely ecumenical, their guidelines include: "We don't try to analyze or diagnose each other (we aren't shrinks) . . ." and "We don't pass moral judgment." "Co-Parenting," by Patricia Zalaznik, Order No. 240, $.20, is especially noteworthy considering it was written before "joint custody" was headlined in the media.

As they are nationwide, they will, upon request, send a list of groups in your area. These groups, however, are primarily Catholic-oriented and most of them meet in churches.

Seminars for the Separated
Boston, Massachusetts

Founded by Dr. Robert S. Weiss, author of *Marital Separation* (see "Suggested Reading"). Open to men and women, Dr. Weiss's group has become the prototype for similar groups throughout the country. Inquiries invited.

Divorce Resource & Mediation Center, Inc.
Cambridge, Massachusetts

Comprehensive services which include support and personal growth groups. Also feature workshops on single parenting, visiting, and single-parent fathers. Private, nonprofit, it offers free information workshops to the public. Also, information and referral service including lawyers, family and social agencies, child guidance specialists.

MANS (Men as New Singles)
Great Neck, New York

While they call themselves a "divorced men's" group, 95 percent of their membership are fathers. Sandy Grossman, the founder, feels that the "men-only" atmosphere is helpful, especially in crisis situations. Fatherhood is regarded as one aspect of manhood; encourages mutual support and self-help. Referrals for private therapy available. Inquiries invited.

For Men Only
YM-YWHA
Scarsdale, New York

Rap groups, social planning, divorce-law reform. Divorced women invited to group once a month.

SINGLE-PARENTS' GROUPS

Parents Without Partners is the best known of the single-parents' groups. Offering a variety of services to both parents and children, individual chapters become known for specialties within a given community. Some are heavy on dances and parties for adults, others have highly varied and structured parent-child programs. The fathers we have spoken to have given mixed reactions to PWP, based on the caliber of the chapter in their area as well as on their individual orientation. Some men have told us that they are simply "not joiners." Others have shied away from what they perceived as "marriage desperation" on the part of its women members. Still others look askance at what they regard as the PWP philosophy; namely, marriage is the ideal state, and every unmarried person should regard remarriage as his or her basic objective in life; past marriages are merely the mistakes from which one learns. It should also be pointed out that many custodial fathers we visited, especially those in smaller communities, have told us that they could never have managed without PWP. Most of the pro-PWP fathers we spoke to were highly enthusiastic about some of the activities; others were indifferent or antagonistic. Very few of them were willing to "swallow PWP whole."

Residents of smaller communities usually have better things to say about the PWP experience than do urbanites, where PWP socials are viewed as one more stop-off on the singles' merry-go-round. Most of the smaller-town custodial fathers regarded PWP as a lifesaver where their children were concerned. The effects of a peer group of divorced children are not to be underestimated in communities where divorce tends to be looked upon with raised eyebrows. Where children are concerned, PWP has been known to lean slightly on the argument of divorce being the greatest boon to a child's psychosocial development. As most of the fathers in our sampling are concerned with tackling the problems of divorce effect on children head on and giving their children the emotional strength to cope with rather than trivialize the experience, they often turn elsewhere for help for their children, although they do encourage friendships within the PWP group.

As custodial fathers are in the minority in PWP groups, they often find themselves in the position of playing "uncle" in parent-child activities composed mostly of mother-children groups. PWP tries to recruit visitation-only fathers for weekend group activity with children, but the visitation fathers we have spoken to do not feel that the "share-the-wealth" philosophy is the most beneficial service they can provide their own father-deprived children.

Also, PWP can have a "let's everybody join hands in a big circle" ambience, which many fathers in our sampling regard as an attempt to gloss over more deeply rooted problems. The fathers are more concerned with upgrading the quality of the relationship with their own children and creating more of a parent–child bond than in fostering the "extended family" atmosphere that PWP promotes.

The visitation father who sees his children infrequently because they live out of state or has other visitation problems may resent the PWP philosophy that he should play substitute daddy to other children when he feels he is being deprived of his own.

Depending upon the individual father's needs and the caliber of membership and services of the chapter in his community, PWP can be an asset or a liability in the life of a single father and/or his children. To some, it can become a "community activity" to which home and family life become subordinate, but in all fairness it must be stated that those who would become dependent on any outside structure would do so within a marriage as well.

In addition to chapter services, PWP holds conventions and seminars for both parents and children, as well as offering group travel and vacations.

We feel it is worthwhile for any father to check into the PWP chapter in his area to see what potential benefits may be available for himself and his children. Contact national headquarters in Washington for the chapter in your area. In addition to newsletters some local chapters may put out, PWP also puts out a magazine called *The Single Parent*. Subscription rates are $2.75 a year for members, $5.50 a year for nonmembers.

In addition to PWP, many communities sponsor single-parents' groups, largely funded by civic organizations. One of them, SOLO, in Portland, Oregon (see Appendix C), puts out an impressive monthly newsletter called *SOLO Center News*. Subscription rate is $2.00 a year.

In addition to those mentioned here fathers should look into whatever services their communities have to offer for divorced parents and children.

CHILDREN

In addition to the single-parents' groups that include services for children as well as parent-child activity, a few innovations have come to our attention, mostly along the lines of children-only peer groups where they are encouraged to confront their problems directly. This, we feel, is among the most constructive approaches for dealing with the problems of children. Although they are limited in region, all welcome inquiries on how to get similar programs started in other areas. We sincerely recommend that every father look into them rather than automatically put the child into individual psychotherapy when problems become apparent. Notable among these are Creative Growth Workshop in New York City; Stepparents Forum in Montreal; Children of Divorce Project in Berkeley, California; and Children Facing Divorce in Denver, Colorado (see Appendix B for details).

The main thing to remember in any form of individual or group help for children is not to push, coerce, or manipulate them in any way to participate. If you remind them that they can proceed at their own pace, and if they don't want to try it now they can always change their minds at a later date, it will then be their decision rather than the manipulation of an outsider.

13

THE VISITATION FATHER

The story makes the round of the New York City cocktail party circuit:

"How do you empty out the Metropolitan Museum in two minutes on a Sunday afternoon?"

"Simple. Just say, 'Will all the divorced fathers with two children kindly step outside the building.' "

According to popular mythology there are two kinds of visitation fathers: ideal and nonideal. The ideal visitation father plays his Bozo the Clown role according to script and, as a reward, enjoys a great hamburger and shake with his child, interspersed with remarks like, "Hey, Dad, these French fries are really *keen.*" The nonideal visitation father, on the other hand, sneaks surreptitious glances at his wristwatch while his child, sullen and bored, stares listlessly at the soggy hamburger.

The visitation, or part-time father, has been spotlighted recently, primarily in the Atkin and Rubin book, *Part-Time Father.* Along with all the other visitation father advice, this book assumes that there is full and flexible cooperation between divorced parents and also that a divorced part-time father wants to be just that. Fathers are rapped on the knuckles for wanting either joint or full custody.

We have spoken to a large percentage of divorced fathers who have full cooperation and flexibility in visitation. Among these are the fathers who can honestly say that their relationships with their children have improved following divorce. There is no stopwatch on their time together. The most liberating aspect of flexible visitation is that it breaks the deadlock of "Sunday with my father" or "Sunday with my children." Thus, the child who plans on attending a birthday party on a particular Sunday knows he or she is free to say, "Can we make it Saturday instead, Dad?" Open visitation is most important for the father whose children have a wide age-span. The rigid Sunday visit for the four-year-old son and twelve-year-old daughter puts a father in a position to plan an activity that is, at best, unsuitable to either child. The Sunday deadlock negates meaningful individual interaction for the father with three or more children. Time alone with one child is achieved at the expense of the others.

Visitation roulette takes several forms. "The handiest unpaid baby-sitter" is the way one father puts it when his former wife suddenly announces a change in her plans. As so many of these men are desperate to maintain contact with the children at any cost, they rarely refuse to obey the finger-snapped command. Another form of roulette is the sudden changeover from the deprived Sunday visit to the mandatory Sunday or full-weekend visit by decree of the custodial mother, not the court. This comes about as the result of one of two situations: The mother has a lover or the father has a lover. In the latter instance the children are used as a means to break up the liaison. Every woman who has ever been involved with a divorced father whose concern for his children goes beyond the check-writing stage tells of repeated plans gone awry at the last minute. In this instance, most fathers attempt to keep plans secret, especially for week-long vacations and three-day holidays. It can tax the patience of the most understanding woman to be faced with the reality that the time she may spend with the man in her life is contingent upon the whims of his former wife. This presents the divorced father with another dilemma. He is often forced to choose between his children and his girl friend. This form of game-playing can be used against the denied-visitation father and the "letter of the law" visitation father with equal effectiveness.

This is another reason why most custody and visitation battles do not take place until six months to a year following the divorce. Unless the father had someone waiting in the wings during the marriage, the former wife's bitterness could have been held at bay. As long as his relationships with women are kept numerous and transitory, the former wife is not threatened. But when he passes through this phase and becomes involved with one woman, unless his former wife has found satisfaction in this area, her feelings of inadequacy and helplessness can be reinforced and she may tend to see herself more as the "loser" in the divorce, even though she may have insti-gated it at the outset.

Thus, two forms of visitation roulette can place the father in the position of baby-sitter on short notice: when the mother finds the children a burden and obstacle to her own love life; or when she wants to use the children to create a burden and obstacle to the father's love life. The cop-out or skip-out father will not be seriously inconvenienced by this. It is the father who wants to maintain mean-ingful involvement with his children following the divorce who will become the victim of visitation roulette. In other words, his parental consciousness is his Achilles' heel. And it puts him at the mercy of both his former wife and the court system.

In between full cooperation and visitation roulette we have the "letter of the law" situation. This is the father who is graciously or otherwise permitted to remain in the presence of his children in an environment other than the mother's home. Some fathers have to have a third party, agreed to by the mother, present. It is these fathers who are envied by the visitation fathers.

Interestingly enough, the righteous "drek-to-dross" advice-givers mentioned earlier blithely assume that every "letter of the law" father is in a full-cooperation situation. Dictums are handed down about telephoning the child frequently, making plans together for future visits, and participating actively in the child's life. Some of these fathers have serious, well-founded doubts about whether birthday cards sent to their children are ever seen by them. These are the fathers who hear the imperceptible click of the extension phone when they call their children, and not all of them are put through when they do call.

On top of all the outside restrictions imposed on the father–child relationship are the inner conflicts of both fathers and children. The guilt of the divorced parent has not been overlooked by the pop psy-chologists. It should simply be stopped at once, they urge. This very instant! The conflicts of the child of divorce are far more numerous than the father's. The child is threatened by positive as well as nega-tive feelings toward the father. He or she has been "abandoned" by the father who does not want to abandon his children. The "letter of the law" child is deprived of a father six days a week and has an imi-tation father on the seventh day. And on and on.

The divorced father, from visitation to custody, has a new parental role to learn. For many of them it means an emerging of the parental consciousness coupled with realistic restrictions on parental functioning. He may be ashamed of his living quarters or, if not ashamed, realize that his children will go stir crazy after more than an hour or two in his cramped apartment. While few men actually get fired because of a divorce, their emotional state is often such that they cannot be considered for promotions or added responsibility. Employers can be expected to be only just so understanding about such situations. Furthermore, the father's job can be jeopardized if he tries to fight legally.

Thus, the divorced father is called upon to shoulder an added parental responsibility at a time when his parental self-image is at its lowest. He has no illusions about the father image his former wife is presenting to the children.

The new parental role thrust on a father as a result of divorce requires an adjustment period on the part of both father and children. Too often, a father is advised to "understand" the problems of his children while attempting to suppress any of his own. This can only create further strains on the relationship. The father must learn to cope with the agonizing "But why can't you marry Mommy again and come live with us?" as well as the "I hate you—you don't care about me!" The advice to the divorced father to encourage his children to express their hostilities, while based on the good intentions of the advice-givers, like all other good intentions, will only pave the road to hell. The father is better off seeking help for his own conflicts and, whenever possible, trying to arrange for services that help his children deal with their conflicts in a nonthreatening environment.

Copping out can take many forms and at least as much of it is done by fathers who spend visitation day with their children as by those who try to avoid it. We hear of taking the children to grandma's every visitation day for a really good home-cooked meal, leaving the children to their own devices while Dad watches the ball game. While children's ties to their father's family—grandparents, aunts, uncles, and cousins—should be maintained for the sake of both children and paternal relatives, when visitation time means only family visits, the father–child bond can only be weakened.

In addition to learning a new parental role, a large number of visitation fathers have another problem to contend with: The child has been stage-directed to ask for money. Even if it's not an outright admonition to "come home with the check in your hand," there are few visitation fathers who have escaped the "Mommy says there are a lot of bills you have to pay," as soon as the car door is closed.

It would be easy for us to list the ten cardinal rules for divorced fathers on visitation day, but doing so would place us in the position of oversimplifying and generalizing various circumstances. We do not feel that everyone would benefit from this; for there are no two visitation fathers whose circumstances are exactly the same. The father who is content with the setup and the father who is fighting for custody are in different situations. The child who is content in his mother's custody and the child who wants to live with his father present different problems to the visitation fathers.

We have, however, spoken to fathers who feel that their relationship to their children, while not ideal, is, at least, functioning at optimal peak in spite of obstacles. Some of them, fighting for custody, have given their children the sense of "we are in this thing together." Some have resigned themselves to the fact that there will be no meaningful interaction until the children have passed the legal custodial age.

LIVING SPACE

The one factor that all these fathers agree upon is the importance of setting up their living quarters, no matter how modest, so that the child feels that this, too, is "home." For those who can afford it and are in a full-cooperation setup, this often means separate rooms or built-in play and sleeping quarters for the children. More often it means sleeping bags.

"What about the father who feels he has no chance of ever having his kids sleep over?" is the most frequent question asked by the novice divorced father. Time and again, the veterans give the same answer. When the children see that their father is planning his home around their needs, the children will regard it as their home as well. These are the men who, somehow, manage to communicate the fact that while, now, they may not be able to stay over, the possibility definitely exists that things may change in the future.

Sleeping arrangements or not, the children must be given the feeling that they are *participating members* of their father's home and not distinguished guests. Meals can be planned together, food shopping can be done together, and cooking can be shared. Quite a few fathers have told their children at the onset of meal preparation, "We may all make a mess of this. I'm as new to it as you are. We can make mistakes together and we can learn together."

No matter how small the living quarters, there can always be one place designated as the "children's corner." This can be a few boxes or shelves that are devoted *exclusively* to the children's belongings: toys for the younger ones, books and paraphernalia for the older ones. Children must have the feeling that there is certain activity that takes place in their father's home and which they can think of as something to be shared with their father. This can be jigsaw puzzles, scrapbooks that are worked on when they are together, or even magazines. Even though the visitation father does not plan to spend all his time with his children in his apartment, the children will have the feeling that their father's home is their home, too.

TIME TOGETHER

Surprises cannot take the place of planned sharing for the visitation father and his children. A picnic, for example, can take on the dimensions of either a Bozo the Clown or a shared activity, depending upon the children's participation in planning. Choosing a picnic area, deciding upon the food, reading the road map (or bus schedule) of how to get to the picnic grounds will be a different experience from that of being whisked off with the announcement, "We're going on a picnic."

Single-parent organizations do not lack in planned activity for Sunday fathers. While this sort of activity can initially help a divorced father over the hump of his own awkwardness in the early stages of the visitation arrangement, being put into the position of overseeing potato races for large groups of children can prevent a father from maintaining an in-depth relationship with his own children. It should be mentioned, however, that for the child who feels that he has been stigmatized by the divorce, the effects of a peer group of other children of divorce should not be underestimated, at least at the beginning. Like visiting grandparents, overorganized group activity can turn into a rationalized cop-out if the father becomes dependent on it.

Holidays and birthdays are times when the wrench is felt most deeply by both father and children. Most visitation agreements provide for alternate holidays with each parent. Therefore, a father may have his children every other Christmas. An elaborately planned birthday party in the custodial mother's home on the scheduled visitation day is not unheard of, nor is the practice of setting out the welcome mat for the father on this day particularly prevalent.

Many fathers arrange beforehand with the children to have a special birthday or Christmas celebration in the father's home although it is no longer the actual holiday. These celebrations can take place between a father and an only child; a father and all his children; or a father, child, and outside guests. Within divorced fathers' groups, members who have children within the same age range make it a point to get together on visitation day. When friendships form among the children, joint activity is planned for some visitation days and birthdays and holidays often are shared.

Assuming that visitation rights are enforced with a minimum of complications and assuming that the predivorce relationship with the children was secure, there is bound to be a period of awkwardness on both sides at the start of the postdivorce relationship with the children. Much has been said about "speaking frankly" with the children and telling them that their pain is being shared. We feel that this can too easily deteriorate into "laying a trip" on the children when they are in need of support themselves. Even if their mother is not speaking to them directly, they cannot help but overhear conversations and get reminders, subtle and not so subtle, that they can't have all the things they used to have "since Daddy went away."

Some fathers have told us they approached the new situation as "something new for all of us. We're all going to feel a little funny in the beginning, and we're going to have to work things out together."

Many newly divorced fathers put a strain on themselves, their children, and the relationship by attempting to be "both father and mother" during the time they spend with their children. Predictably, they end up as neither. Overly defensive about the stereotype and slogans that inform them that "men can't nurture; men don't have the same way with children that women have," they become pseudo-Mrs. Portnoys about dressing them warmly, feeding them enough, and obsessively searching the children's faces for a sign that all may not be perfect bliss in their lives. These men feel that anything short of total happiness in their children's lives indicates total inadequacy in their father role, their provider role, and the very basis of manhood itself. More than one father has assured us that he always bakes bread on visiting day. If bread-baking is an activity you and your children can share together, fine. Otherwise, forget it. You're not a male madonna!

The divorced father with only one child is, understandably, concerned about his relationship with that child. In fact, it is the one-child stereotype that is inevitably spotlighted in the now-famous hamburger scene. Woe to the multichild father, one of whose children is a pizza addict! The multichild father deadlocked in a "letter of the law" situation does run the risk of bypassing the one-to-one relationship that is essential to any child's feeling that at times his father is available "just for him." A twelve-year-old might be reluctant to express doubt about his ability to form friendships in the presence of younger brothers and sisters. A four-year-old may feel like a tagalong at activities planned for a ten- and twelve-year-old. Some fathers have turned the age-span of several children to everyone's advantage by planning "one child" visitation days when the other(s) had plans of their own for that day. This alleviates a major source of guilt on the part of both father and child. The preteen who wants to take part in a neighborhood or school-based activity on visiting day is relieved of a feeling of betrayal toward his or her father, as the father will feel that the visitation day deadlock will not interfere with the child's social development within the peer group. He tries to make sure, though, that each child gets a fair share of one-to-one days.

The father who has minimal visitation and is fighting for custody has an added responsibility for openness in dealing with his children. Talking about the future is important. Even though these children are being deprived of time spent with their fathers, it is essential that they be made aware that the day will come when their relationships with their fathers will be free of constraints. One father we know makes the Sears-Roebuck catalog an important part of the time he spends with his ten-year-old son and eight-year-old daughter. They talk about fixing and furnishing the home they will eventually share. The boy has a fairly adequate knowledge of carpentry tools; the girl has the color of her room all picked out (yellow) and has already enlisted the cooperation of her father and brother in helping her paint it.

Realistically, however, many fathers are aware that the custody battle (if a court battle is taking place) will continue until the youngest becomes eighteen. Not every divorced father has the security of an open, warm relationship with his children. These men are not deluding themselves that their former wives' bitterness or indifference to them will not have a corrosive effect on the relationship as well as on the child. This is where our postcustodial fathers (those whose children are over eighteen) become most adamant to the younger fathers with their admonition to "Hang in there!" The divorced father whose visitation days are characterized by a sullen, accusatory "You're a bad Daddy!" from a four-year-old or a smooth, casual "You know, Dad, you were really quite a bastard for walking out on

Mother" from a fifteen-year-old constantly has to fight the temptation to throw in the towel. This is where the older fathers reiterate constantly, "Tell your children they are entitled to their feelings, but as they get older they may see things differently." No matter what happens, they advise, assure your children that you are their father, you will always be their father, *and you are their father even though they may hate you now.*

The men who have sought some form of therapy for themselves, from private psychotherapy to informal rap groups, report the most success in seeing a hostility-based relationship with the children metamorphose into one based on openness and trust. These are the men who, wisely, learn that they have to deal with their own feelings before they can expect to deal with their children's.

The visitation father is concerned about aspects of his children's lives that go beyond time spent together; namely, what is happening in the lives of their children when they are not with them. School reports and medical care are two major areas of concern to the non-custodial father and, frequently, areas where the mother may decide to withhold information. The father in the early days of divorce would do well to have these areas covered in the custody agreement.

So far, we have been describing the visitation father who lives within commuting distance of his children, and although we know several fathers who regard three hundred miles each way to be "commuting distance"—and make the trip every week—geographic distance does create additional problems for the visitation father. Ideally, this father will have open telephone and mail arrangements. If his children have moved to another area, he should keep them advised that their friends and family ask about them. When he does visit, he can make his hotel or motel room his base of operations, and they can plan from there. He should also make it clear that his home is his children's home, and there is a place for them when they come to visit.

Inasmuch as most visitation takes place on weekends, the question comes up, especially for those fathers whose children sleep over: What about the women in their lives? In this, as in other aspects of divorce, there are the inevitable two schools of thought, liberated and conservative. Although we are aware of the swinging faction, or "Everybody snuggle under the covers together," the fathers in our sampling are adamant that this aspect of a relationship is to be kept separate from their time with their children. The subject is discussed fully in chapter 16.

The father who is living with another woman would be wise not to attempt to keep this fact in the closet. Some fathers have told us that they have had their children stay over when their girl friends slept over but made it clear to the children that she was someone special and that their relationship with her would be on a continuing basis. This can cause stress, especially among preteen and teen-age children. If their mother has been casual about having a series of men sleep over, this can cause added problems to the children, and more than one father has told us, exasperatedly, about his attempts to explain the difference to his children between special relationships and promiscuity. Many fathers who are painfully aware of the custodial mothers' casual attitude toward their own sex lives in the presence of the children have made a special effort to keep this area of their lives separate from their relationship with their children.

Also, the father who is fighting for custody is particularly vulnerable in this area. Like it or not, children are pumped for information by their mothers.

No matter what the visitation situation is, all the fathers agree on one point. That is, it must be made clear to the children in attitude and action that because you are not living with your children does not mean that you have abandoned them.

14
JOINT CUSTODY

Joint custody is the most recent innovation in changing custody trends and represents the smallest group of all child custody arrangements. It is the most widely spotlighted, however, especially inasmuch as most fathers view it as a way out of visitation deadlock. As rare as it is, joint custody seems to be provoking some near-violent reactions, especially from those who are advocates of one-parent rule. Even the element that tends to be rather casual about divorce effect on children can be threatened on a gut level by the idea of children living in two homes.

Two of the most ardent foes of joint custody are Estelle Rubin and Edith Atkin, authors of *Part-Time Father*: "Some fathers want their children who live with their mothers to feel that dad's house is also the children's home, i.e., that they have two homes. This insistence only emphasizes that the children live in a divided world. Your [the father's] home can be a place where they feel comfortable, accepted, loved—in short, where they feel *at home*. But their home is at their mother's."[1]

Rubin and Atkin are further quoted to the effect that children need the security of one home. Among proponents of divorce, the "mommy's home" is beginning to take on the Norman Rockwell quality once attributed to the two-parent home.

Doris Sassower, who pioneered the concept of joint custody as a viable legal alternative to one-parent rule, presented the following description of the average, mother-custodial home: "She [Sassower]

1. Claire Berman, "Father's Day Is Not Just on June 20," *New York Times*, 18 June, 1976, p. 38.

also queried whether a single parent having sole custody does not subject the child to just as much shuttling and uncertainty as retention of the father as joint custodian would mean. Between working and dating the wife is likely to leave the child with sitters about half the time. . . ."[2]

Joint custody has a number of variations, and we will try to list all of them. First of all, joint custody does not necessarily mean split custody, where one or more children live full time with each parent. The most prevalent form of joint custody is when children spend equal amounts of time living with each parent. We have heard of a few cases of joint custody where the children remain in the family house, with the parents taking turns living there. Of course, switching homes on a weekly or biweekly basis is viable only when both parents live in the same community.

At this writing, seven fathers in New Jersey are bringing a class suit against the state of New Jersey. One of their aims is that joint custody be considered a viable alternative to the present custody laws. Not every father is looking for an alternate-weeks setup.

Joint custody in the case of Charles Cornell and his two children means that the children can spend summer vacations with him and that he has telephone privileges. Cornell lives in New York State and his remarried wife lives in Florida. Should his children, Charles and Rochelle, decide they want to live with him permanently, they may do so by going before the judge and declaring their wishes. Cornell will not have to petition his ex-wife into court.

But to most fathers, joint custody will mean that their children will be able to spend weekends and holidays with them and be functioning members of their households. Equally important, these parents feel, will be their right to consult with school and medical authorities with full-parent status.

The motives behind joint custody can be as numerous as the joint situations themselves. Fortunately, most parents do have their own parental consciousness combined with concern for the children's well-being as their prime motivation. These are usually full-cooperation cases, where the court is rarely brought into the decision-making process.

The courts, as is common knowledge, still assign custody to mothers about 95 percent of the time, and because of holdover

2. *Family Law Reporter*, 1 FLR 2708, 26 August, 1975.

attitudes, fathers are legally pushed into the role of "visiting" parent. But well over 90 percent of custody arrangements never involve the courts; they are worked out between separating parents and their lawyers.[3]

The above quotation is taken from an article by Charlotte Baum, who has been sharing custody of her three children with her former husband for the past five years. This decision was made when Ms. Baum and her former husband each realized that neither one wanted to become a visiting parent or assume a less active role in the lives of their children.

Another newspaper article has the following to say about joint custody:

Besides being a new idea, joint custody may also be just a paper pact, as Professor Foster [law professor at New York University and chairman-elect of the American Bar Association's Family Law Section] and others suggested, a balm for guilt that parents, especially mothers, feel when pressured by society to fight for a custody they are unable or unwilling to assume.

Several lawyers, including Brenda Feigen Fasteau, who practices in Manhattan, recalled handling such cases. "Sometimes," Mrs. Feigen Fasteau said, "their term 'joint custody' is a cover for a man having real custody and a woman not wanting to lose face by giving up custody."

Other times joint custody may be a father's compromise. For example, Allen, a 35-year-old Los Angeles accountant, said, "I'm fighting for joint custody because I don't approve of my ex-wife's swinging lifestyle.

"To get complete custody," he said, "I would have to prove her an unfit mother, to bring her drinking and drug problem in the court, which would destroy her in the eyes of the children."[4]

Joint custody, like full custody, has its full cooperation aspect as well as court battle circumstances. When it is obtained as the result of courtroom proceedings, full custody was invariably the first choice of each parent. Doris Sassower feels that joint custody will be

3. Charlotte Baum, "The Best of Both Parents," *New York Times Magazine,* 31 October, 1976, p. 45.

4. Georgia Dullea, "Joint Custody: Is Sharing the Child a Dangerous Idea?" *New York Times,* 24 May, 1976, p. 24.

the wave of the future in custody settlements. As we mentioned before, the Molinoff case has received the most publicity. Although each parent initially wanted full custody of the two boys, Dan Molinoff feels there is now a full-cooperation situation. The Molinoffs have an elaborate schedule of splitting three- and four-day weeks, alternated so that the children spend an equal number of weekends with each parent. Molinoff feels strongly about the split week rather than a Monday-to-Monday situation, which characterizes most joint custody. Marilyn, Dan Molinoff's former wife, was quoted in the *Christian Science Monitor* (May 5, 1975) as saying she agreed to the arrangement reluctantly and is personally bitter about it but does not feel that it has harmed the children.

The women's movement has not shown itself to be particularly sympathetic to the concept of either joint or full paternal custody *unless this arrangement has been initiated and approved by the mother.* Doris Sassower epitomizes the early women's movement dream of combining a successful career and family life. We watched her blithely accept a Distinguished Woman's Award for her contribution to feminist causes, the legal profession, and encouragement in career planning for young people, surrounded by her three beautiful children. "Feminism," said attorney Sassower, "should convey the concept of shared responsibility and freedom from stereotypes. In general, feminists have not been sufficiently liberated to leave the care of their children to their father."[5]

Daniel Molinoff gives us some insight into his initial joint custody experience:

> The State Supreme Court justice who presided over our case thought sharing custody was madness. "Why do you want to stay home even part of the time?" he said. "You're the man!"
>
> Most of my relatives and friends also thought I had made the wrong decision. Most of the uncles and aunts, none of whom had been divorced or separated from their children during their marriages, thought Michael and Joel were "better off with their mother. Mothers take care of children," they said, "not fathers."
>
> My friends didn't like the idea of my having custody either, but for different reasons. Most of the men I knew were angered by what I was doing. The married men, who were not taking as

5. Jo Ann Levine, "Parents Agree to Joint Custody," *Christian Science Monitor,* 5 May, 1975, p. 18.

active a part in the upbringing of their children as I was, saw my arrangement as a threat to their marital tranquillity, to the system, to Manhood. . . . As for the women I knew . . . they couldn't understand why I'd want to cook and clean for my children . . . other women, including neighborhood mothers and my sons' teachers, considered me the village villain. They looked at joint custody not as a benefit to the children. More than once I was told, "You're just being vindictive."[6]

As Tim, a divorced father fighting for custody, puts it, "The divorced father has come full circle—from the bastard who saddles his wife with the responsibility of bringing up the children to the bastard who wants the responsibility of bringing up the children."

The finger-shaking experts have no hesitation in condemning the concept of joint custody:

This reluctance [to approve of joint custody] stems from the notion, supported by psychiatric evidence, that a child needs the security and stability of first, one primary residence and . . . second, one custodial parent to make the major decisions on his upbringing. . . . From the standpoint of the child, the situation is one of divided authority or what's called the double bind—it's a dangerous situation for a child. . . .[7]

In other words, the "roll over, play dead, pay up" syndrome appears once again. Divided authority is something that is bound to exist in a two-parent household unless one parent studiously neglects the parental role. The teddy bear as bulwark of stability in a child's life is usually cited as the chief argument against joint custody. But several joint-custodial parents we have spoken to feel that giving up one parent could conceivably be a greater sacrifice on the part of a child than giving up one teddy bear.

Clint and Nina have had joint custody of Carol, nine, and Deren, seven, for three years. Their apartments are four blocks apart. The children spend alternate weeks with each parent, but there is no rigidity about their schedule. Clint will not hesitate to take the children to the dentist during Nina's week if she has another appoint-

6. Daniel Molinoff, "After Divorce, Give Them a Father, Too," *Newsday*, 5 October, 1975.
7. Dullea, "Joint Custody."

ment, and vice versa. Each apartment is well equipped with the children's belongings; only bicycles go back and forth.

As with so many joint-custody arrangements, neither lawyers nor the courts were involved. During the marriage, there was a slow transition from role-deadlocking to role expansion in household and child-care chores, as Nina's interests took her out of the house more and Clint revised his working schedule as a free-lance editor to allow him more time with the children. One might say that, realizing it or not, Clint and Nina were preparing the children for a joint-custody arrangement even before they themselves were aware of it.

There are several aspects of Clint and Nina's arrangement that make it more advantageous for both parents and children than most conventional two-parent households. Foremost among these is the level of cooperation between Clint and Nina and the openness with which they deal with the children. Even before the separation, the children were told that Clint was going to move into an apartment that would be their "other home." They were assured that they would remain in the same school, have the same friends, and see both sets of grandparents, as they did before. When asked about the arrangement, the children usually reply, "Sometimes I don't know which address to put down in school," and "I forget which toys are at Mommy's and which are at Daddy's."

Frequent family meetings characterize the arrangement. Holidays, vacations, and any schedule changes are discussed during these meetings, where the children are encouraged to express their preferences and feelings.

Speaking to Clint and Nina separately, we could not help but be impressed by the high regard with which they spoke of one another in the parental role. Each feels it is the personality differences of the other that are beneficial to the children. Clint describes himself as being basically a homebody, and the time the children spend with him is based on stay-home activity. Nina, on the other hand, is a dynamic person interested in activities outside the home and wants the children to participate in them with her. Clint feels that this contrast enriches the lives of the children.

Both parents feel that the shared schedule releases them to pursue their own interests, which, in turn, benefits the children. Since the separation, Clint has revived his childhood interest in music and plays in a jazz quartet while Nina has taken up sculpture. Each parent feels that the expanded horizons of the other results in a higher caliber of parenting. They each credit full financial cooperation as the basis of the success of the arrangement. Their incomes are about equal; neither one has ever asked the other for money for the children's day-to-day needs; medical bills are divided equally. Each one feels that the children are getting the benefit of two stable, if not luxurious, homes.

Clint keeps his relationships with women separate from his time with the children. Nina, on the other hand, involves the children in the relationship she has with a divorced father who has weekend custody of his two children. We did get the impression that if Clint had his way, Nina would limit her relationship with this man to the time when she did not have the children, but he takes the point of view that this is one more difference in their respective personalities from which the children may benefit. There was never the problem, which happens so frequently with newly divorced couples, of the plethora of sexual partners immediately following divorce in a desperate attempt to forestall feelings of inadequacy or of attractiveness to the opposite (and, occasionally, the same) sex.

If there were a Norman Rockwell illustration of the ideal joint-custody family, it would feature Clint, Nina, and their children. Not only such handsome young parents and beautiful children but such a bond between each parent and the children as well are rarely observed in more conventional family setups.

It is not our intention to portray either the father-only or the joint-custody household situation as the new models for covers for the women's service magazines. Clint and Nina represent that rare instance where each has achieved expansion in personal development as a result of their divorce. They are supportive of one another in the parental role. Inadvertently, Clint and Nina have become reluctant role models for other couples within their social milieu. Unfortunately, the results have not always been similar.

Ben and Sarah's marriage followed the same course as Clint and Nina's, at least outwardly. Each couple had two children in close succession shortly after the wedding. Each started out with conventional role-deadlocking, husband as breadwinner, wife as breadbaker and child-caretaker. Sarah and Nina met in the same consciousness-raising groups. Each woman regarded the role-deadlocking as her prime obstacle to personal growth and development. Each began revising division of labor within the home. Each husband, reluctantly at first, eagerly later on, became more involved with the details of household and child care in addition to their jobs. Each wife felt that "the world out there" held promise for her.

Clint and Nina were the first to make the break. Wary at first, Sarah, after seeing the positive results in Nina's life, began to believe her own salvation lay in imitating Nina.

The results were disastrous. Ben was summarily dismissed from the family home; an apartment was found for him several blocks away. The Monday-to-Monday schedule was set up, for which the children had neither adequate preparation nor warning. The children were informed that they would be living one week with each parent in much the same tone that they would have been informed that no, for the last time, they could not stay up and watch the late show on television.

Sarah's sexual liberation lasted for about a month, at which time she concluded that approximately thirty male chauvinist pigs had used her as a one-night stand. The children were showing signs of severe disturbance. Sarah's only consolation, after Ben refused to move back in with her was that "Ben was regressing emotionally."

Like so many women whose feminist consciousness was raised higher than their job qualifications, Sarah made the "liberating" step from wife to daughter, taking the children to live with her and her parents in a distant community. Her rationale was faultless—better schools and neighborhood, the relationship with their grandparents, small-town life, etc. Ben, in the meantime, returned to the original family apartment, which he later came to describe as a tomb. Sarah refers to the divorce as the best thing that could have happened to her and the children. The children state it differently. "I *hate* divorce[1]" says seven-year-old Jeffrey. "I *really* hate it," echoes nine-year-old Hilary. She will hurl a bowl of cereal across the kitchen to emphasize her point.

In joint-custody situations, the children are often at the mercy of the postdivorce adjustment made by their parents. When Sarah's unrealistic fantasies did not materialize, she got back at Ben where it would hurt him most—his relationship with the children. "Those children were my life," Ben explains, as he tells us how role expansion in household tasks and child care deepened his emotional ties to the children. Probably more than in any other custodial arrangement, the quality of the divorce and how the children are helped through it is the keystone of the workability of the arrangement.

Oddly enough, endorsement for joint custody comes from one

quarter where it would least be expected. Patricia Zalaznik's excellent pamphelt, "Co-Parenting" (see Bibliography) states: "My former husband had the opportunity to be more than an occasional parent, and one of his strong desires is to continue being a relevant father. . . . The children have a *real experience* with each parent."[8]

Ms. Zalaznik is to be credited for her awareness of the pitfalls of joint custody as well, but her writing has a quality about it that happily avoids the "Goodie Two-Shoes" character of most Advice to Divorced Mumzies and Dadzies.

Joint custody, understandably, will work most smoothly when it is the decision of the divorcing parents rather than the courts. Charlotte Baum's article in the *New York Times Magazine,* referred to previously, is the first national article to deal with the subject. According to the author, it has been working satisfactorily *for both parents* for five years. We kept reading and rereading the article looking for the part where Ms. Baum and her former husband had helped the children through the divorce process. We couldn't find it. The author did, however, describe anxieties experienced by the children, then aged nine, seven, and four. Although she describes the youngest as displaying the most "surface calm," she says of him: "But every night he crept into my bed, and no matter how many times I took him back to his room, he always managed to wake up beside me in the morning."[9]

The article provoked one outraged letter to the editor in which the writer expressed the opinion that the article sounded more like a discussion of joint property than joint custody.

But, wherever "the best interests of the child" are concerned, those best interests are subject to interpretation as to the best interests of the people defining the best interests of the child. Thus, it is no surprise to read the following excerpt from an article that appeared in Ms. magazine about a plan involving approximately twenty-five families in the New Haven, Connecticut, area who participate in equal-time custody.

> We've found that children involved in the New Haven Plan are more independent than most, and free of the nightmare fear that they may be abandoned. Abandonment seems less likely to children when there are two parents and two homes that wel-

8. Patricia Zalaznik, "Co-Parenting," Conference of Separated and Divorced Catholics, Boston, Mass., n.d.

9. Baum, "The Best of Both Parents," p. 46.

come them. Their dual homes force them to develop more ways of interacting with a variety of people.[10]

We are firmly convinced at this point that if there were parents who advocated children sleeping with boa constrictors, arguments accompanied by clinical research would suddenly appear proving that not only did sleeping with a boa constrictor improve the child's self-image, but schoolwork, peer relationships, and psychosexual adjustment would be far above the norm for his or her contemporaries who were still making do with a worn-out teddy bear.

Granted, joint custody can present enough problems when full cooperation exists between custodial parents. Neither lawyers nor custody-fighting fathers are under any illusion that a court battle for joint custody will be any less bloody than a conventional custody battle. Commenting on the Molinoff case represented by Doris Sassower, the *Family Law Commentator*, referring to a "bitterly contested custody proceeding," states:

> She [Sassower] advanced the "still seemingly radical idea that fathers should have equal rights of their infant children." . . . The current egalitarian movement with its emphasis on eliminating male/female stereotypes might be sympathetic to the idea of equal custodial time. The burdens of parenthood are shared equally and not according to notions based on the sex of the parent. Of course, the arguments against joint custody would also apply to equal custodial time. The idea expressed in Goldstein, Freud and Solnit, *Beyond the Best Interests of the Child*, that one parent should have complete control of the child would naturally be opposed to the equal time custodial time arrangement.[11]

Sheldon is the father of two boys, eleven and eight, and a girl, five. For two years he has been trying to get his visitation orders changed. Currently, he is allowed visitation on three consecutive days per month. He is trying to get this changed to one-day-a-week visitation. Shel is living in a furnished room in order to support the family home (where his former wife's lover has moved in). His children want to be

10. Marcia Holly, "Joint Custody: The New Haven Plan," *Ms.*, September 1976, p. 71.

11. "Equal Custodial Time—A Revolutionary Concept," *Family Law Commentator*, 4 no. 4 (July/August, 1975): 1.

with him, but as he puts it, "They go stir crazy after an hour at my place." While most heated arguments regarding joint custody come from parents, judges, lawyers, and psychologists, Shel was advised on joint custody from still another source.

His eight-year-old son asked him, "Dad, why can't we live one week with you and one week with mother?"

15

THE FULL-CUSTODY FATHER

A divorced father has custody of his children under one of three circumstances. Basically, they are (1) full cooperation, (2) reluctantly or with no choice, and (3) following a court battle. Each category has its ramifications and variations, and we will try to cover them all.

Representing the lowest percentage of custodial fathers, full cooperation generally indicates the agreement between both parents, prior to the divorce, that one or all of the children will live with their father following the divorce, usually in the family home. Under these circumstances, which come closest to ideal, the divorce itself as well as future living arrangements are discussed openly with the children prior to the separation. It is these children who are the most fortunate inasmuch as the divorce experience itself has been effected with a minimum of trauma to them.

Another, less frequent full-cooperation circumstance is when the father gets custody anywhere from one to three years after the divorce. These are fathers who wanted full custody from the beginning but settled for flexible, open visitation arrangements that almost equaled joint custody. The children had a place in their fathers' homes, and there was open communication between the parents about decisions affecting the children. The way this father gets custody is usually by a change in the custodial mother's life-style: sometimes a dramatic career advancement, more often a remarriage. In either instance, custody of the children, she feels, could jeopardize either her career or remarriage, and she is usually glad to hand over custody. As the postdivorce father–child relationship has usually been secure in these circumstances, the change is welcomed by both father and children.

Another instance of full cooperation might better be called *reluctant* full cooperation on the part of the mother. The children, most often teen-agers or preteens, simply announce that they are going to live with their father. Period. These mothers are often genuinely hurt at what they can only perceive as total rejection on the part of their children. Most of them, however, deserve credit for acting in the best interests of the children. Others are embarrassed at losing face but are very much aware of what a court battle could do to them, especially if there is an outspoken teen-ager involved.

The no-choice or reluctant category of custodial fathers also has its subdivisions. While most fathers we interviewed initially described their situation as full cooperation, as the stories unfolded, it became clear that their custody started out as no-choice. Their wives simply announced that they were leaving, and that was that. In some instances, the child-raising role proved to be too much for the woman, and having had premarriage problems triggered off as a result of the strain of disappointment in the marriage, the woman's mental and emotional state deteriorated to the point where she was simply unable to care for the children. These situations are, understandably, most traumatic for both fathers and children.

Most no-choice situations were preceded by pathetic attempts on the part of the husband to keep the marriage and family intact. These attempts usually included a history of years of marriage counseling combined with individual therapy. This situation is best exemplified in Albert Martin's book, *One Man, Hurt,* in which the author describes his own and his sons' futile attempts to preserve the marriage and family.

Needless to say, it is the no-choice situations that can throw a father into a sudden panic at the prospect of full responsibility for home and child care in addition to his career. These men often undergo crisis situations for about six months, during which time they tend to withdraw. It is also these men who usually emerge on top of the situations, having developed deeper senses of self-confidence in the process, especially if they had been role-deadlocked within the marriage. Like the custodial mother, the custodial father who feels he is unable to manage alone with the children following the divorce tends to become marriage-desperate within a short time. Like hasty first marriages, these hasty remarriages have a high attrition rate, and divorces are even more prevalent among second marriages than among first.

The lowest percentage of custodial fathers is found among the men who obtained custody after a prolonged court battle. This is the category that will have to be scrutinized most carefully, as there is probably more dichotomy here than in any other paternal custody situation. Most people envision custody battles as sensational yellow-journalism stories involving millionaires, each parent battling for the custody of the millions, using the children as the excuse for the money. In these cases, the custody battle begins with the first visit to the lawyer.

In reality, most fathers do not attempt to gain custody until approximately six months to two years following the divorce. For some, the feeling is strong that full custody is the only way they feel they will be able to maintain any relationship with the children, especially when visitation roulette involves a bullet in every chamber. Unfortunately, not all these fathers have a realistic concept of what full custody entails and, should they win, would have a difficult time adjusting to the responsibilities.

But most postdivorce custody battles are begun when fathers observe the progressive deterioration in the level of the care the children are receiving at the hands of the custodial mother. In some instances, a poor postdivorce adjustment on the part of the mother may manifest itself in alcoholism and/or drug problems. In others, it is the "swinging" life-style that causes concern to the fathers, although they are quick to point out, "What she does is her own business, but, please, not in front of the children." Others observe what they regard as callous indifference on the part of mothers toward their children, although they may be quite circumspect in their personal lives. Still others, willing, and sometimes eager, to look the other way where their former wives' parental shortcomings are concerned, realize they will have to take action when the children's chorus of "We don't want to live with Mommy any more" begins.

Another form of custody battle is the father who wins custody by virtue of his lawyer's fitness in vilifying his former wife rather than by his own fitness as a parent. This caliber of father will not hesitate to employ the lowest forms of visitation roulette. We heard about one such father who did not want to speak to us. The children were in boarding school, and we did get flak about his former wife's "highly immoral life-style." This is the type of man who can afford to and will produce photographs of his wife in bed with a lover.

But for the average divorced father whose parental concern outweighs any desire to vilify his former wife, the decision to fight for custody is not an easy one. They are too aware of what public mudslinging will do the children's self-image, although they realize this may be the only legal weapon available to them. Today judges are, fortunately, not as willing as they were twenty-five years ago to instantly place the "unfitness" label on a mother because of one instance of infidelity. Unfortunately, the only cause for a mother to be given an instant unfitness label today is a proven lesbian life-style. Of course, this is prejudicial, but as can be expected, gay rights leaders are busily gathering evidence that a child growing up in a home with an open, loving, lesbian relationship has a far better chance of a normal, healthy, psychoemotional development than he or she would have in the custody of a rigid, uptight father who is closed-minded and tyrannical in matters like sexual orientation.

Feminist circles have spotlighted the Risher case, in which Mary Jo Risher, a former Baptist Sunday school teacher and PTA president, began living with her lover, Ann Foreman, three years ago. The joint household included Ms. Risher's two sons and Ms. Foreman's daughter. Ms. Risher's older son, Jimmy, is now eighteen, married, and a father himself. By his own choice he went to live with his remarried father, who is trying for custody of the younger boy, Richard, nine. Richard has expressed the desire to remain with his mother in the reconstituted household.

Ms. magazine described the situation: "They [Risher and Foreman] consider themselves 'just like a heterosexual family,' with the difference that 'neither one of us depends on the other to fulfill any type of role.' Theirs is a permanent commitment. They are each other's insurance beneficiaries, they have a joint checking account, and they co-own property. According to several psychologists, the children have an exceptionally loving stable family life."[1]

Quoting Richard's father: "I have a wife who could be there to attend to [Richard's] needs twenty-four hours a day. There would be a father and mother image portrayed that he could model himself after. There would be outdoors and sports, vital to a young boy."[2]

1. Lindsy Van Gelder, "Lesbian Custody: A Tragic Day in Court," *Ms.*, September 1976, p. 72, © Ms. Magazine Corp., 1976. Reprinted with permission.
2. Ibid., p. 73.

The article continues: "Cross-examination[3] revealed some interesting facts about this model Dad. He once broke Mary Jo's nose during a fight. He has a drunken driving record. Between his marriages he hung out at singles' bars, had sex with several women, and was accused of impregnating an eighteen-year-old."[4]

Frankly, we would not want to be faced with the decision of having to award custody of any child to a lesbian mother in a loving relationship or a wife-beating father with a record of drunken driving. And while it is no more our place to say that homosexuals are unfit for child custody than it is anyone's place to say that fathers are unfit for child custody, we did feel that the windup of the article managed to overlook a discriminated segment of society in the child custody question: "In general, the lesbian custody picture is still a bleak one, and to women like Mary Jo, other women's victories can't compensate for the loss of a child."[5] The article ends with an appeal for contributions to Ms. Risher in her custody battle.

We have yet to find any mention about bleakness in the father-custody picture in a feminist publication. However, as noted before, the women's movement endorses father custody when it is a result of husband-dumping or full cooperation with the divorced mother. As to a father wanting custody without the mother's approval, spite, vindictiveness, or a desire to get out of support payments are the only motives which the feminists will attribute to these men.

We have no intentions of denying that there have been and are fathers fighting for and obtaining custody with spite and/or economics as their prime motive. We have heard of fathers fighting for children as a strictly financial maneuver. This is prevalent in the higher income brackets where the father's parental consciousness manifests itself in the hiring of a competent housekeeper for the times between boarding school and camp. But in general, the argument that a man fights for custody strictly to get out of child-support payment does not hold much water. With the current trend away from awarding alimony, a divorced father could get off much more cheaply with support payments to his ex-wife than he could in maintaining a home for the children.

The increasingly unpleasant reality in mother custody is that the children can be used to obtain support payments in addition to welfare. Quite a few payment-responsible fathers have bitterly

3. By *Ms.* magazine, not the courts.
4. Ibid., p. 73.
5. Ibid., p. 73.

complained that their support money rarely goes for the support of their children. Of course in the case of the complete skip-out father, the mother can usually qualify for welfare for herself and the children. As we have pointed out before, the welfare state is expanding to include more and more members of the former middle class.

Probably the most ambivalent statement that could be made about the custodial or would-be custodial father is that he "wants" his children. Unquestionably, the full-cooperation custodial father could be said to *want* his children, as it could be said that his former wife *wants* the children to remain with him. Also, the no-choice custodial father unquestionably *wants* his children, although his first preference would have been to have the family remain together.

It is in the case of the custody-fighting father that the expression "he wants his children" can be most ambiguous. Most of these men have told us that, ideally, they wished they could have felt secure about the well-being of their children in the custody of their mothers. For every custodial father we have spoken to who describes himself as managing smoothly, we have spoken to at least three who admitted that they "didn't know what they were getting into." They have pleaded with us over and over again, "Please, tell everyone you speak to, don't fight for custody unless you are sure you can handle it."

Not every father-awarded custody story we heard has the proverbial storybook ending. We heard of one case from a lawyer whose client had been fighting for custody of his sons for six years because of their mother's alcoholism. When he finally obtained custody, the children were, in the lawyer's words, "basket cases," who had to be institutionalized. This lawyer was quick to point out that the client, a fireman, subsequently remarried and started a second family and leads "a solid, secure family life."

As easily as a custodial father can be looked upon with raised eyebrows, it is the mother who has voluntarily given up custody who is regarded as the pariah. Headlines invariably zero in on the mother who "skipped out" to "do her own thing." This focus on the "who-gives-a-damn?" mother manages to overshadow the divorced mother whose relinquishing of custody was based on a heightened sense of parental responsibility. We were fortunate enough to speak to some of these women, and thanks to a full-cooperation visitation agreement with the custodial fathers, their postdivorce relationship with their children remains stable and secure. Most of these women based the decision on the fact that the children would be happier in the family home with their fathers. Others told us that the children's relationship with their fathers was such that they considered the father to be the primary parent. Others have agreed to split custody based on the children's preferences. Some have retained custody of very young children, with the understanding that these children may change custody any time they express the desire to do so. Others frankly have told us that they advised their former husbands, "OK, I've had them long enough. Your turn now."

By and large, both these types of women are the women about whom it can honestly be said that they have "the best interests of the child" at heart. These are the women who, along with the men who express the desire for prime responsibility in child-raising, should be receiving society's support rather than its censure. These are the women who bow to their children's preferences although they may, at first, be shocked and hurt by what they regard as rejection. These are the women whose parental consciousness has been raised higher than their feminist consciousness.

Still, the question remained in our minds: How did the custodial father manage raising the children by himself? There was no one answer. Frankly, we rejected the swinging-divorced-bachelor-Dad image and concentrated our efforts on the custodial fathers whose prime interest was to establish stable homes for themselves and their children. We went into the homes of about twenty-five fathers and spoke to about fifty more, sometimes with their children present, sometimes not. These men ranged in age from early thirties to late fifties. Occupations ranged from carpenters and maintenance men to doctors and professors. Incomes ranged from about $13,000 a year to $50,000, with $20,000 being the median.

As interviewers we had the preconceived notion that the higher the income level, the smoother the father-headed household would run, based on the logic that the higher-income father could more easily afford household help. We couldn't have been more wrong. The stability of the home was in direct proportion to the degree in which the family members operated as a team. The men who had household help seemed to fall into one of two distinct categories: the guilt-gift father, and the responsibility-oriented father. The guilt-gift father was characterized by viewing his parental role as one of buying the children gifts and relieving them of any form of responsibility for the running of the household. The responsibility-oriented father viewed his parental role as developing his children's sense of responsibility and self-sufficiency, which he viewed as the keystone of a child's self-respect. Among the guilt-gift fathers, the housekeeper's prime function was to negate the necessity of any of the children having to lift the proverbial finger in the running of the household. Among the responsibility-oriented fathers, the housekeeper's task was to see that the children did the chores as well as driving them to and from after-school activities.

Hal is an example of a guilt-gift father. He obtained custody of his three children, seventeen, fifteen, and eleven, by "default," when his wife remarried. Hal always had open visitation, and the children spent weekends with him prior to his gaining custody. Although he used to visit them frequently when they were in their mother's custody, he described the atmosphere in his former wife's home as extremely tense. Hal bought a new house when he learned that he would get custody. When the children joined him, he tried to set up a chart to assign household tasks to them. He immediately received an outraged rebuttal from his older son: "That's the sort of thing *Mother* always did."

Hal's children have learned that they can use their three mother-custodial years as an effective weapon against Hal, and they don't hesitate to do so. Hal describes himself as "exploited" by his children. He never felt that his former wife was, in any way, an "unfit" mother, although he did make reference to her "top sergeant" tactics.

Jake, on the other hand, obtained custody of his three teen-aged children after a tedious court battle. Unlike Hal, he never had the assurance that his children were getting adequate care in his ex-wife's custody, especially when her drinking problem intensified. Because of the chaotic environment the children experienced in their mother's custody, Jake is convinced that they must have order in their lives and learn that they are responsible for the condition of the household. A family conference is held every week, and household chores are "up for grabs." Suzanne, the live-in nineteen-year-old household assistant, is a sophomore at a nearby college. Her schedule is taken into consideration in coordinating household tasks, and she takes part in the family conferences. The children are being brought up to regard Suzanne not as a maid but as a young person who, like them, is planning for a life career.

Material goods is another category where we felt the higher-income father would indulge the most heavily. Again, we were wrong. Jake's children, all at once, asked him for ten-speed bicycles. Jake explained the economic facts of life to them and told them that in order to maintain the cabin in the country, they all would have to watch expenses. The kids were referred to *Consumer Reports* for ratings on ten-speed bicycles. They're now looking for secondhand ten-speeds, or the possibility of trading in their three-speed bikes with money they've earned themselves to make up the difference.

Stuart, who has had custody of six-year-old Jonathan since he was eighteen months old, except for the year when Jonathan lived with his mother and her new family, is a guilt-gift father whose income level does not match either Hal's or Jake's. Stuart has misgivings about having "retrieved" Jonathan from his mother, stepfather, and half sister. Whenever Jonathan asks about his "little sister," Stuart promises to buy him a new toy. When Jonathan tries (and usually succeeds) in worming another toy out of him, Stuart announces, in a martyred tone, "I'm being blackmailed."

Arrangements for child care, especially for very young children, is the prime concern of any single working parent. Options differ in large cities and small towns. While having family living nearby gives any single parent a sense of security should an emergency arise, upward, lateral, and sometimes downward social mobility make the "extended family" a thing of the past in all but certain ethnic groups. But even in the absence of an extended family, neighborly and community concern can be strong. Many smaller communities have licensed baby-sitters. These are usually women with large homes and families of their own who have been licensed by the community to care for other children. These women are characterized by their affinity for children rather than college credits, and they do provide a decidedly homelike atmosphere. While most of these baby-sitters' services are used for after-school care, some accept very young infants for all-day care as well, and from what we have heard, are quite adept at preparing formulas.

Most fathers spoke highly of the baby-sitters, although one voiced the objection that his three-year-old daughter watched too much television, and expressed the desire for something more on the order of a preschool learning environment. As to the question of possible child neglect or downright abuse from a woman who has too many children to take care of, one can be assured that these fathers go into the sitters' homes every day, and if anything were amiss, they would recognize it immediately. Also, these sitters provide more of a peer group environment for the children rather than a mother–surrogate child relationship, which is beneficial to preschool-age children.

Another advantage the smaller communities have to offer is the neighbor relationships. The question was put to us as to how these fathers are regarded by the community at large. Here again, it depends on individual circumstances. When the father remains in the family home with the children, he is considered something of a hero in the town. This is especially true in a full-cooperation or no-choice father-custody situation. While Daniel Molinoff, the joint-custody father, has much to say about having been regarded as the village villain initially, we have found that the full-cooperation or the reluctant-custodial father manages to escape the label of 'the bastard who took those children away from their mother." The ideal custodial-father situation, especially in a smaller community, is when both parents, prior to the divorce, tell the neighbors that the children will remain with their father. It is when secrecy surrounds the situation that fuel is given to gossipy neighbors. A father who moves with his family to a new community will be regarded suspiciously at first. Most fathers in our sampling reported genuine concern on the part of the community, even to the extent of neighbors going to the father and telling him that the children were to come to them immediately in case of any emergency. Similar cooperation is reported on the part of school officials. The father who goes to a principal and states his desire to be kept informed of the progress of his children, emotionally as well as academically, is usually regarded as something of a hero to the school as well.

Attitudes toward divorce vary from one community to another. It is in the larger cities that we tend to think that divorce is accepted more casually, if it is given a second thought at all. It is also in the larger cities that divorced people tend to congregate. Initially, this might give the impression that both divorced parents and children would have an easier adjustment living in a large city, but it is an erroneous one, especially for the custodial parent. While it is true that a child of divorce will be more the rule than the exception in a large city, the very indifference toward divorce applies to services and concern for children as well. It would be hard to imagine certified baby-sitters taking care of other people's children in addition to their own, given the limitations of most city apartments. The anonymity characteristic of city life cannot coexist with the neighborly concern (which can, let's face it, easily deteriorate into snooping) found in a small town. Most of the fathers we spoke to felt that their children had a strong sense of community identity as a result of the father-custodial situation.

It is in these smaller communities that single-parent organizations play such a large role in the lives of both fathers and children. Parents Without Partners is a completely different experience in a small town from what it is in a large city. It is the father whose children are in the minority because of the divorce who speak most highly of the children's activities provided by the single-parent organizations. Also, in these communities, there is an almost "barn-raising" quality about the way single parents band together for mutual cooperation. Custodial fathers with daughters especially are concerned that an adult woman be available to their daughters, especially during preadolescence. The subcommunity provided by single-parent organizations is especially meaningful in smaller communities, where the one-parent family could feel left out.

Visitation problems encountered by the custodial father are almost the complete opposite of those of the visitation father. Of course, when there is full cooperation, visitation and telephone problems are minimal. However, because many mothers move to a different area following the divorce, frequent visitation becomes impractical, and these fathers make every effort to maintain frequent telephone contact between the children and their mothers. The no-choice custodial father's major problem is getting his wife to agree to talk to the children on the telephone. Instilling in the children the sense that their mother cares about them is not an easy task for these fathers.

Stuart had a problem when Jonathan was four. Until his former wife remarried she would have nothing to do with Jonathan, on the telephone or off. Jonathan hadn't seen his mother since he was eighteen months old, and one morning he announced to Stuart that he didn't want to go to nursery school any more because "Billy says I have no mother."

It is to Stuart's credit that he took the morning off from work to go to the school. He brought along a picture of Jonathan as an infant, sitting on his mother's lap. Patiently, he explained to Billy and the other children in the class that "everybody has a mother and father" and that Jonathan, too, has a mother, "but she doesn't live in our home." He also told Billy, "I've never seen your father, but I know you have one because everybody has a father." He also prevailed on the teacher to ask the children to bring in photographs of themselves with one or both parents.

Fathers and Custody

Men who have obtained custody after a court battle have a different visitation problem, especially if the children have requested paternal custody. Often, these mothers are unable to cope with the children for any length of time. In these cases, the children are often reluctant to visit their mother, and if there is more than one child in a family, each may insist that the others accompany him or her. Jake, for example, pointed out to his children that their mother's visitation rights included having them sleep over at her home. The children balked and told him, "For a couple of hours, OK, but overnight—no way." Jake tries to explain to the children that although their mother is an alcoholic, she is on her way to being rehabilitated. But he has no intention of forcing the children to be with their mother.

Of course, many fathers feel that their custody is in jeopardy, as it has been said that "no custody decision is ever final." When private detectives are involved, these men feel they are living like fugitives and have to keep their homes superclean, their children superneat, and that they, themselves, must lead an almost monastic existence, inevitably putting a strain on both father and children.

The custodial fathers we chose to include in our sampling tended to take the same attitude about their personal lives that the visitation and joint-custody fathers did: "Keep your love life separate from your time with the children." They did, however, point out that if they were to have a woman sleep over, she would have first been introduced to the children, and it would be made clear to them that this woman was someone special in their father's life.

One of the aspects of the custodial father that we were most eager to learn about was his ability to cope with household management. Logically though, the answer to the question "How do these men manage with the cleaning and cooking?" was based on the extent to which they were involved with household management prior to the divorce. A surprisingly large number were more involved than either the women's service or the macho magazines would lead us to believe. In the full-cooperation as well as some of the dumped-husband cases, many men had been sharing household and child-care tasks, especially if their wives had been working during the marriage. In the custody-after-court-battle situations, the men had taken full household responsibility prior to the divorce simply because their wives were "unable to cope" for one reason or another. For the men who had to cope with a woman who couldn't cope, the departure of their wives made the difference between a stressful and a stress-free environment for both husband and children. A strong case has been made for divorce as beneficial to children using the exact reverse situation, where the father is regarded as the prime source of tension in a home, and his departure is all that is necessary to create a harmonious household.

We are not trying to build a case to the effect that every disappearing act on the part of the mother automatically guarantees the happy father-only family. No one is more aware of this than the no-choice custodial father whose marriage had been characterized by role-deadlocking. In addition to nonexistent preparation for the children that their mother was leaving, these men were utterly devastated at the prospect of home and child care in addition to their jobs. This anxiety is especially accentuated in the income brackets where household help is out of the question. This is also the category in which so many men see remarriage as the only solution to their problems. This is the same category where, oddly enough, these men emerge six months to a year later very much on top of the situation. These are the men who usually seek help from divorced-fathers' and single-parents' groups. Many of them report a sense of self-esteem that had never before been experienced in their lives.

On the other hand, we have spoken to men who were fully confident of their ability to take full custody prior to the actual custody award but later felt that they didn't know what they were getting into. They are the men who strongly urge others to know what they're getting into beforehand and, if at all possible, to seek the help of services and organizations that will help them prepare for the full-time father role (see chapter 12). As many fathers fighting for custody spend most of their noncareer time embroiled in legal details, often fighting *pro se*, the veteran custodial fathers express the apprehension that these men may be falling into the same trap as the bride-to-be—planning the wedding in meticulous detail but having no preparation for the reality of married life.

Anxiety on the part of a custodial father often manifests itself in an oversolicitous concern for the petty details of housekeeping. Wax buildup on the kitchen floor and tattle-tale gray in the sheets must be avoided at all costs. These men are especially defensive if they are greeted on all sides with "But, of course, a man can't run a home the way a woman can." As in the case of mothers, divorced or otherwise, this fanatic preoccupation with neatness can only be detrimental to the children's sense of security and stability.

The homes we visited ranged from superclean to the nth degree to supercasual to the same degree. It was our observation that the relaxed approach to housework occurred in direct proportion to the ease and security of the total home environment. The fathers who described themselves as having been the primary parent prior to the divorce regarded the details of housekeeping as decidedly secondary to the quality of the environment they were providing for their children. Many of the newer custodial fathers (six months or less) explained to us that they were in the process of organization, and schedules were beginning to work themselves out. We had many an interview interrupted by a four-year-old (and, sometimes, a few of his friends) stopping for "a quick snuggle with Daddy" on his way out to play. And if Ira or Win happened to be in the path of that snuggle, we got it too.

It is our impression that the quality of the father-only household is based on two key factors: how the divorce was presented to the children, and the postdivorce mother–child relationship. We visited several split-custody homes, where one or more children lived with each parent. When split custody is a result of the children's request, it is, understandably, more open and cooperative for both parents and children. The child living with one parent who knows the household of the other is available to him or her is, indeed, fortunate.

What about the father whose custody is in jeopardy? This problem is most severe for the father with younger children, where court discrimination is strongest against father custody. There are custody situations that have involved a series of child-snatchings back and forth between the parents and both father and children feel they must live like fugitives. The most seriously threatened custodial father, however, is the one whose former full-cooperation wife changed her mind about custody a year or so after the divorce. This happens most frequently when the mother's postdivorce life receives a serious setback, and child custody could mean both support and welfare eligibility for her.

Another instance where father custody can be considered precarious is when the mother is being institutionalized. The current trend toward shorter incarcerations coupled with heavy drug therapy and outpatient care has many fathers seriously concerned about the future of their children. Courts do have a tendency to reverse an "unfit" decision if the mother promises to obtain psychiatric care. Many psychiatric social workers who have told custodial fathers they saw no hope for the rehabilitation of the children's mothers have made it abundantly clear that they would never testify in court to that effect.

While there are many fathers who consider their custodial positions precarious, to say the least, there is probably an equal number of fathers who regard their noncustodial positions as being just as precarious. We heard about Maynard from Doug, one of our joint-custody fathers, who made it clear to us that Maynard was not about to speak to us.

This is his story: Maynard was divorced from his wife five years ago. At that time, his wife took their two children, a boy of six and a girl of four, to a distant city, where she remarried. Visitation was made difficult for Maynard, a dentist, and he shortly resigned himself to a childless life. He was in an income bracket where wine, women, and song, in addition to support payments, presented no financial problem to him. Five years later, shortly after her third marriage, Maynard's former wife called and told him she was on the verge of suicide; he would have to take the children. Maynard, at this time, considered himself a total stranger to the children. He was terrified at the prospect of full responsibility for two pre-teen-agers who, he was convinced, "were screwed up beyond repair."

Maynard had called Doug for advice, but Doug explained that his own custody situation was very different. The first thing Doug suggested was that Maynard get himself a full-time housekeeper and get into a divorced fathers' group—fast.

In so many of the "I Was A Male Mommy" books, there is a glib casualness about the pragmatic aspects of home and child care that is not borne out by the reality of the situation. Many men do find the adjustment difficult, at least initially. They question their ability to manage, and often blame themselves for the breakup of the home. They may tend to hover over their children looking for symptoms of psychological disorder and devote more effort to creating a pseudo-psychiatrist–child relationship than to a father–child relationship. A recent magazine article described this situation:

> Donald Pasternak is divorced and has had full custody of his children [a ten-year-old son and an eight-year-old daughter] for four years. . . . He ponders over remarriage and worries about the reaction of his children, particularly his daughter. He's joined groups and tries to build ties and come out of his isolation. . . . He realizes the loving and caring he provides is not mothering, though he finally concluded that he provides them with the basic stability of what a woman would have provided. . . . He is a single father by choice. His wife has not

gone to the Great Beyond, nor has she committed crimes against the State or the Heavenly Father. The Pasternaks made the decision that would best suit their family needs and have stuck by them.[6]

Bob Bernstein is a father who has custody of his seven-year-old son, Eric. His four-year-old twin daughters are in their mother's custody. His situation was described as follows:

> Most pressing . . . was the lack of time, for getting through the domestic chores and for free hours for himself. "From school, I go to my next full-time job, and being a parent is a full-time job," he said. "Sometimes I feel envious of divorced fathers whose ex-wives have custody because at night they can pick up and go. But there are so many positive things about having Eric. When I talk to other divorced fathers, one of their big complaints is they feel alone in their apartment. I don't have that problem at all."[7]

We reiterate: The only homes we went into were by invitation, as were the father-children teams we met outside of the home. These men were, by and large, proud of their situations and the way they managed, and they unquestionably represented the more successful adjustments of custodial fathers. We are not trying to deny that there are problem-ridden father-only households, nor are we trying to present father custody as the solution to all divorce problems involving children. It is not our intention to replace the myth of the maternal instinct with the myth of the Dandy Daddy.

We would like to say, however, that the degree of stability we encountered in these father-only homes as well as the caliber of the parent–child relationships struck us as being unusually high.

Higher, in fact, than in a good many two-parent households we've visited.

6. Florence Fois, "The Single Father: A Case Study," *Women's Week* (New York), 8 November, 1976, p. 3.

7. "The Single Father: A Full-Time-Job," *Newsday*, 9 September, 1975.

16
DATING, REMARRIAGE, STEPPARENTHOOD

According to statistics, divorced men and women have the highest remarriage rate in their respective age groups when compared with the widowed and never-married.

> More divorced men remarry than women (75 percent compared to 66 percent), especially if they have custody of the children; it's easier to marry a housekeeper than to hire one. Divorced women hold better odds of hearing wedding bells than single women of the same age. . . . By the time both groups reach 40, the divorcée's odds are 2 out of 3, while the single woman's odds of marrying have dropped to a lousy 1 in 7.[1]

We have no statistics on the number of remarried custodial fathers, although the above statement would lead us to believe that more custodial fathers remarry than remain single. Therefore, the custodial fathers in our sampling probably represented the minority because we were emphasizing the single-father state.

The most explosive divorce situation is the one where one partner has a remarriage scheduled almost immediately following the divorce. This type of father is not likely to fight for custody; he is probably more likely to establish a new relationship than maintain ties with his children. We have spoken to only one father whose second

---

1. Carol Saline, "Who's for Seconds?" *Philadelphia*, September 1976, p. 183.

wife was waiting in the wings prior to his divorce. He has custody of one son and is fighting for the other.

Statistics do show that divorce rates for second marriages are higher than for first, the rationale being that people will not hesitate to undergo divorce a second time.

We did find a higher percentage of remarriage among the fathers in our sampling who were fighting for custody, some of whom had started second families. From what we could gather, with the exception of the father mentioned above, none of these second marriages were "waiting in the wings" situations, and most of the men obtained or began fighting for custody before their second marriages. In these circumstances, the wives were fully aware that the men were fighting for custody and that they would probably be called upon to play the stepmother role. Some remarried fathers told us that what they were looking for in their postdivorce courtships was a willingness on the part of their future wives to bring up the children. Disillusioned by the apathy of their first wives toward child care, the men placed the desire for home and family, or lack of career ambition, among their priorities in choosing a second wife. This attitude will, of course, be denounced by the women's movement, but it must be realized that there are women who find fulfillment in the homemaking role whose outside jobs, if any, will be secondary to the wife-and-mother role.

Most of the men in our sampling were unmarried and had no immediate plans to remarry for a variety of reasons. A lot of them were simply afraid to try again. Others felt they were financially in no position to marry, believing that too heavy a financial burden would be placed on the shoulders of their second wives. Most of the fathers with full custody said they hoped there would eventually be a "lasting, committed relationship" in their lives, but felt that, at least for the time being, neither were they emotionally ready for remarriage nor could they foresee anything but further strain on their children, themselves, their wives, and possible stepchildren as a result of remarriage.

Relationships with women will present more problems for the child-oriented divorced father than it will for the legendary womanizer. Perhaps we can differentiate between the two by referring to the father who is more concerned with the result of his former ejaculations than the one who is fanatically obsessed with his future orgasms. We got the impression that the man who was concerned with his fatherhood identity escaped the impotence anxiety of the indifferent father, who tended to regard his visitation rights as an obstacle to his (largely fantasized) Casanova propinquities.

Thus, the concerned divorced father is faced with another dilemma. If he is not satisfied with a Bozo the Clown relationship to his children, chances are he will not be satisfied with the proverbial "Slam, bam, thank you ma'am" relationship to women—at least, not for very long. It is no secret that promiscuity has been used as an attempt to escape one's feelings of inadequacy about desirability to the opposite (and sometimes the same) sex, as alcoholism has been used to escape facing feelings of inadequacy as a person. In each case, a higher consumption rate is used in an effort to offset a diminishing satisfaction level.

Fortunately for most divorced people, this phase is passed through relatively quickly. For those who cannot integrate their sex lives into their total life picture, the tragedy can be compared to that of the alcoholic parent—the children become victims as well.

Where does all this leave the concerned visitation father, the father fighting for custody, or the joint- or full-custody father? Some of them answer, "No place." Of these three general categories of divorced fathers, the visitation father has the toughest problem, especially if visitation roulette characterizes the divorce. Even when visitation follows the letter of the law, Saturday or Sunday is usually the assigned day, both of which are considered prime dating time. Much has been said about the dating problems of the divorced custodial mother, the most familiar cliché being, "As soon as a woman is divorced every man automatically assumes she is an incurable nymphomaniac."

The visitation father who has rejected (or been rejected by) the singles' bar scene does not have a problem meeting available women unless he has voluntarily chosen a hermitlike existence. His problem is more one of how to get started once he has met them. In many ways, he is in more difficulty than he was during his high school days when he wondered what would happen when he asked a girl to a school dance. He has to reenter the dating scene with a number of handicaps. He has changed, male–female relationships have changed, and the social scene has changed. If he is financially responsible for his children, he feels financially handicapped. Although women may be more willing to accompany him to his apartment instead of an expensive resturant much sooner than during his bachelor days, he may be ashamed of that apartment. He may find that glib chatter about independence for women is used as a not-too-effective cover-up for marriage desperation. In addition to the emotional turmoil created by the divorce, his anxiety about the children, and his financial problems, he may feel that his job performance is at somewhat less than optimal peak. He may have discovered the emptiness of a series of one-night stands but fear any serious involvement. The age and life-style of a woman also has to be taken into consideration. If she has never been married, he may feel she cannot understand his problems. If she is divorced, she may be bitter about her former husband and feel that all men get away with murder in divorce. If she has custody of her children, she may be, if not exactly marriage-desperate, understandably anxious that her children have a stable male figure in their lives, especially if her own ex-husband is not that concerned as a father.

The man who had difficulty in getting his own visitation rights enforced can feel guilty about becoming overinvolved with someone else's children. He may feel disloyal toward his own children and fear becoming a fixture in the lives of another woman's children. Many divorced fathers have told us that the custodial mothers they had been dating have let them know in no uncertain terms that a breakup of the relationship would create problems for her children.

The problem of establishing a relationship is felt most keenly by the divorced father whose visitation is contingent upon the snapped-finger commands of his former wife, formal court orders notwithstanding. These men feel that they are at the mercy of their former wives where visitation is concerned. The father whose visitation is almost nonexistent at least knows where he stands and can plan for his own time. The father whose visitation can be changed at a moment's notice is afraid to plan. As has been mentioned earlier, more than one father who had his visitation curtailed almost completely while he was living a monastic life suddenly has found a strong awareness of the need for an improved father–child relationship on the part of his former wife when it became known that he was dating.

Rivalry between a man's female friend and his children is getting more and more attention in the media. An article in *Viva* warns, "He may be the apple of your eye, but courting his kids is no picnic."[2]

When last-minute date-breaking becomes a pattern in courtship, tempers can fly. Resentment on the part of a woman toward a man's children can begin long before she has ever met them. He can feel

2. Judi Miller, "Dating Someone Else's Daddy," *Viva*, January 1977, p. 64.

torn between her and his children; she can accuse him of being at the beck and call of his former wife.

Divorced fathers fighting for custody are often reluctant to become involved too deeply with women, especially during the custody attempts. Discretion may be in order, especially if the former wife has set private eyes on him.

Because of his preplanned schedule, the joint-custody father is in a more flexible position to become involved with a woman. If joint custody is interpreted as the children spending weekends with him, and his former wife has an active social life of her own, there is usually some degree of cooperation about taking the children on different weekends so that he is free to make plans involving himself and his friend only. The joint-custody fathers we have spoken to usually plan to keep their children and their female friends separate, at least until some degree of commitment concerning the future has been established. This does not necessarily reflect an attitude of Puritanism on the part of these men. They simply feel that their time with their children belongs exclusively to them, at least at the beginning. Others, whose joint-custodial former wives are more casual about their dating relationships, feel that this is already a problem area for the children and one which they don't want the children to have with both parents. Still other men feel that if their children become attached to the female friend, it may cause problems if the relationship is short-lived.

Many joint- and full-custodial fathers maintain an "open house" atmosphere in their homes, encouraging frequent visits from both their own and their children's friends. This, they explain, will make the transition smoother if they should become involved with a woman than if the children were to regard their father as exclusively their own property. Sharing friends, then, is one of the advantages of membership in a single-parent organization. Many custodial fathers attributed their success in running a stable one-parent home to Parents Without Partners for helping them create this open house atmosphere.

Many of these men also credit the single-parent organizations with helping them gain a sense of self-esteem in all areas of their lives. During their marriages, some of them were belittled in their husband, father, and community roles. They now find themselves looked up to not only by their own children but by the single-parent community as well.

Most of the full-custodial fathers in our sampling had strong opinions regarding remarriage—mostly against, at least for the foreseeable future. They admitted that during the early days of custody when the most minor task seemed a major hassle, marriage was regarded as the panacea, at least in coping with day-to-day tasks. They all quickly realized that instant solutions could create long-range problems. They also felt that the relationship they had worked so hard to establish between themselves and their children could be strained by a new marriage. Some of them stated that marriage would only create another upheaval in the children's lives and put their new wives in the position of outsiders as well.

They admitted that they would like to be married but realized that their requirements would place too much of a burden on the women they married. A childless woman, they know, might not be able to step into the situation suddenly and deal with children who may still have problems resulting from their pre-father-custodial experience. A woman with children of her own would, understandably, be concerned with the needs of her own children. These fathers realize that they would be expected to spread their emotional energy to their stepchildren as well, possibly at the expense of their own children. In addition, many custodial fathers are still carrying a financial burden for their former marriages—if no alimony or "maintenance," as it is currently called, then in the form of medical bills or psychiatric care. They also realize that their new wives would have to work to help support their first wives.

Once the initial anxiety of "How will I ever manage?" becomes transformed into "We are managing," the father's self-image takes a turn for the better. Happily, many of them now state that they "never had it so good."

The attitudes of fathers toward single-parent groups is not shared by all single mothers. While many custodial fathers regard these groups as freeing them from the need to remarry, a great many of the mothers join these groups with the specific goal of remarriage in mind. Bitterness and resentment is expressed by the women who feel that the men are eager to establish a "sugar-borrowing" relationship with them but seek more romantic attachments elsewhere. The fathers feel that remarriage is the primary goal of the custodial-mother membership of these groups and the men express apprehension that a gesture of courtesy, such as opening a car door, could be interpreted as a proposal.

Social activities are an integral part of the single-parent groups. While many of the fathers feel obligated to put in an occasional appearance and make it a point to ask the women who have been helpful to them to dance, it happens that the women with which they eventually become involved romantically are often not members of the single-parent organization in which they participate. One reason for this may be that too much of a "cousin" type of relationship tends to evolve among group members.

Still, once a relationship has been established, the major question for custodial fathers is, "What about having women sleep over?" Most of them answer, "Only when the relationship is serious and the children know she is someone special in our lives." Others state flatly, "Not when the children are there." A November 1976 television program entitled "Life Styles" had a panel discussion of single-custodial parents. It also featured a film clip of teen-age custodial children. Virtually all the children expressed the opinion that they wished their parents would keep this activity outside the home. "After all," stated one thirteen-year-old boy who lives with his father, "we know what's going on and we feel that we're not wanted."

But whether the situation is one of visitation, joint custody, or full custody, more often than not a time comes in the life of a divorced father when a relationship with a woman will become an integral part of his life, whether or not a marriage is planned. Today, the question of how to introduce the woman in his life to his children has the same implications as the question of "bringing her home to meet Mother and Dad" had twenty-five years ago. How this meeting will go depends to a large extent on the ages of the children, how secure they feel in their relationship with their father, and how communicative the father has been with his children about his friendships in general. Images of kiddies and Daddy's New Friend hitting it off together on a picnic exist more in the realm of fiction than on picnic grounds.

The children who feel ambivalent about their mother will experience added guilt if they have an affinity toward father's girl friend; the child living with a custodial mother is often pumped for information.

Stepparents Forum is a newsletter (see "Suggested Reading") aimed not only at remarried parents but at men and women who are dating divorced parents as well. They grapple with the issues of stepparenthood rather than gloss over them. Dixie deVienne, the editor, is the second wife of a custodial father. Although her stepchildren are now grown and no longer living at home, her interest in the step situation continues, as she feels that this subject will have to be confronted not only by parents who face divorce but also by people who have never been faced with either marriage or parenthood.

According to Ms. deVienne, the step situation exists at least as often outside a remarriage as within one, and stepparenthood, if the relationship should reach that stage, will have to be tackled long before the remarriage takes place, whether or not one or both parents are custodial. She regards "living together" arrangements as part of the step picture.

"Take the surprise element out of the step situation," cautions Ms. deVienne. Too often, she feels, fathers approach the question with crossed fingers and a sense of "If we don't admit there will be a problem there won't be a problem." This method is about as reliable in the step situation as it is in contraception. Dad's lauding the praises of kids to girl friend and vice versa with all the missionary zeal usually reserved for deodorant commercials on television can guarantee only one effect: It won't work.

One of the aims of *Stepparents Forum* is to do for the image of Wicked Stepmother what the divorced father's movement is trying to do for the image of Divorced Father as Total Bastard. In reality it doesn't require marriage to a divorced father for a woman to earn the exalted status of Wicked Stepmother; all she has to do is exist. Dixie deVienne refers to this situation as the "step-other." Generally the "other woman" in the life of a father is about as revered in the eyes of a postdivorce wife as she is in the eyes of a predivorced wife. Mature, civilized understanding on the part of a divorced wife usually exists only when her own postdivorce life has proven satisfactory all around. Therefore, the wickedness of the "other woman" is in direct proportion to the emotional state of the former wife as well as to her own relationship with the children. It is the lament of many "step-others" that they are vilified by former wives in direct proportion to their concern and desire to establish a relationship with the children, *not the reverse.*

Of course, the "waiting in the wings" second wife or living-together girl friend expects to have the usual labels of home-breaker and other synonyms for *bitch* applied to her and is, presumably, prepared to cope with it. But it is the women who have become involved in relationships with fathers several years after the divorce has become final who most bitterly resent the vilification they receive at the hands (and mouths) of first wives. These women are the least prepared for it, and Mom often has no qualms about using the children as couriers to the step-other about her feelings. As it is, then, often the problems of divorced fathers become the problems of their female friends.

As we mentioned before, the custodial father whose children are involved in his social life will have an easier time smoothing the way for both his children and his dates. The father who has devoted all his time to his children to the exclusion of others will have problems, as will his children, when a woman is suddenly brought into the picture. The casual, offhand approach doesn't really work. The children should be told beforehand that their father does have a new friend and maybe, sometime soon, they'll all spend some time together.

If little kids are simply not the woman's bag, a lot of grief could be avoided if this fact were acknowledged early in the relationship. If the father makes it clear to both the woman and his children that there is no existing law which states that they must love one another, he might succeed in circumventing the irreversible hatred that is bound to occur when one human being is presented with a long list of reasons why another person is so wonderful.

This is one circumstance where a rap group for children could be extremely helpful, whether or not the father is custodial or whether or not a marriage is planned. Breaking up a relationship with a woman "for the sake of the children" will have the same effect as trying to hold a marriage together with Scotch tape and bubble gum "for the sake of the children." Each will result in guilt on the part of the children and resentment on the part of the father, to say nothing of the woman. We would almost go so far as to prescribe a Wicked Stepmother rather than a martyred father as being the lesser of the two evils in the life of any child.

One of the most realistic planned marriages we heard about involves Jake, the father of three teen-agers, and Elizabeth, his fiancée. Jake and Elizabeth have been seeing one another for about a year and a half. His oldest son has made no bones about it: "She is not going to be my mother," he says. Elizabeth has made it equally clear that she is a successful career woman and is not about to don the proverbial ruffled apron. Jake frankly admits that he is apprehensive about the marriage but has tackled this problem as he has tackled each problem since he took custody. He has open meetings with the children and Elizabeth and takes the approach that "we are five people who are going to undergo major changes in our lives." Jake plans on moving into a new home when he and Elizabeth marry because he does not want Elizabeth to feel like an outsider moving into a home that was planned and decorated without her. "The new home," he explains, "will be the team effort of five people. We have to set it up so that the needs of five people are met. Five people will be involved in the planning."

The subject of stepparenthood promises to spawn almost as many books as there are guides to happy marriages. At least as much conflicting advice will be found in them. Looking into the step situation before it becomes imminent is advisable, especially for the childless partner. Quite a few divorced fathers' groups have a second wives' membership; some of them have auxiliary second wives' groups.

At this writing an organization called Remarrieds, Inc. (see Appendix B) with headquarters in Santa Ana, California, has twenty-two chapters in thirteen states. According to Howard Samuelson, the director, Remarrieds derives a large percentage of its membership from former Parents Without Partners members. (PWP automatically disqualifies membership upon remarriage.) According to Samuelson, people join Remarrieds for one of two basic reasons: (1) They feel remarriage carries a stigma and don't want other people to know they are remarried; and (2) they remarry and have a need to make new friends, to continue the same type of activities offered by single-parent groups, to develop contacts with couples having similar remarriage problems, and to remain part of an organization. We don't know what percentage of the membership of Remarrieds includes custodial fathers.

The problems of remarried fathers do not stop at the step relationship of his children and his second wife. In fact, the opinion has been set forth that they may start there. The problem of divorced men paying alimony and child support for children whose custody they want receives more than understanding on the part of the second wife. It also receives a good portion of her income if she is working, and she usually is, especially if she has custody of her own children. This is the major concern of the second-wife membership of divorced fathers' groups.

The halo of motherhood that surrounds a first wife in the courtroom is not applied to second wives, especially if they represent the father's second family rather than his first. Many second wives are bitter that alimony and support payments have been known to increase upon the father's marriage to a working woman. Visitation roulette takes on an added dimension when a second wife accuses her husband of stooping to his first wife. Sometimes a custody-desirous father feels that a second marriage will increase his chances of obtaining custody, especially if it was denied him on the grounds that he could not provide a proper home for the children. Disappointment often follows very closely; many children have been placed in institutions and foster homes by court order when the custodial mother has been proven unfit beyond any doubt, rather than awarded to the father and his second wife.

Custodial or not, the divorced father stands a good chance of marrying a custodial mother. The father who feels he is being deprived of his own children is bound to undergo a conflict about being a father to someone else's children. Somehow, mythology and folklore have conspired to spare the stepfather the "wicked" label. Hamlet, it must be remembered, did not have the highest opinion about the man his widowed mother married, whom he considered responsible for his mother's widowhood in the first place. But the "something rotten in Denmark," namely Hamlet's stepfather, never quite reached the state of notoriety reserved for Cinderella's step-mother.

A three-year study for the National Institute of Mental Health, headed by Dr. Paul J. Bohannan of the Western Behavioral Sciences Institute at the University of California, showed a lack of father–child conflict in stepfather families. Dr. Bohannan is quoted: "Stepfathers simply don't believe that they're doing that good a job and they are perpetuating a negative image of themselves."

According to Rosemary Erickson, a sociologist who participated in the research: "It looks as if it's more important to have a father, whether it's a stepfather or a natural father, than to be raised in a mother-headed household."[3]

The divorced father who has ruled out remarriage or another form of committed relationship because of the children faces the same problem as the mother who has devoted her life completely to her children. The children do grow up, and the "empty nest" could leave a void in a man's life as it could in a woman's.

3. "Study Finds Stepchildren Content," AP, *New York Times,* 28 November, 1976, p. 83.

While we can understand a father's reluctance to become seriously involved with a woman immediately upon gaining custody and wanting to devote all his time to his children, he will be doing both himself and his children a disservice if he treats all his relationships with women as closet situations.

A prime responsibility of parenthood is to give children an understanding of what committed relationships mean among adults. And what better way is there for accomplishing this than by setting examples?

17

CONCLUSIONS: THE EMERGING PARENTAL CONSCIOUSNESS

There is overwhelming evidence that prejudice exists against fathers in a custody situation. A man has very little legal recourse when he is cut out of his children's life altogether. The importance of father–child interaction has been established beyond any doubt. We have seen father-only households that provide a stable environment and a sense of security and well-being for the children.

There is one major difference between the divorced-father prejudice and most other forms of prejudice. As a general rule, when we speak of prejudice and discrimination against a group—be it ethnic, racial, or physically handicapped—we tend to speak in terms of deprivation and hardship suffered by that group. The prejudice against divorced fathers, however, creates deprivation and emotional hardship for more than just the fathers: While it has been said that children are often the victims of divorce, a major con-tributing factor to the victimization of these children is discrimination against their fathers by our legal system combined with the studious avoidance of the problem by those who are not (or not yet) involved.

There is an inherent danger in offering panaceas for prejudice, and that danger is creating reverse prejudice. For our society to do a sudden flip-flop in the blatant discrimination against fathers and automatically assume every woman is unfit to be a parent because she is female will accomplish nothing.

In this book we have presented the case for divorced fathers and children. We have shown those fathers who are coping successfully in the one-parent household to the benefit of themselves and their children. It would be too easy to fall into the trap of saying that every man will be successful in the single-parent role. Conferring instant sainthood on a man simply because he became a father would perpetuate the same form of child abuse that now exists because of the instant sainthood designation awarded to mothers. Creating a reverse custody situation that would perpetuate a lack of interaction with the mother similarly could not possibly benefit a child.

Another trap we must avoid is to assume that a man suddenly develops a parental consciousness because he is considering divorce. Divorce no more creates an indestructible father–child bond than marriage automatically creates an indestructible husband–wife bond. We must face the fact that the father–child relationship that exists in many conventional families is on about the same level as a number of mother–child relationships—hopelessly dismal. These relationships will not improve, either within or outside of a marriage, until each parent reaches his or her potential as a human being. At one time, marriage was credited with guaranteeing this growth potential. Today, divorce is being credited with the same thing.

For a while, among certain factions of both the men's and the women's movements, there was talk about a "paternal instinct." If we were to create a paternal instinct as we did a maternal one, all we would achieve would be another rationale to justify placing the fate of a child in the hands of a possibly incompetent adult.

We will have to place our attitude toward the maternal instinct under closer scrutiny. In reality the maternal instinct has about as much to do with parental consciousness as applying for a marriage license has to do with the stability of that marriage. No one ever speaks of a maternal instinct among cockroaches; it is reserved for humans and other animals that nurture their young. Nevertheless, it is a phenomenon that exists as long as the young are helpless and dependent, and often beyond.

Among humans, the maternal instinct becomes deadly when it is used to keep the young helpless and dependent. This same maternal instinct, when perverted, leads to the demoniac force that creates the overly possessive mother who would rather see her child dead than emerge from the dependency state.

Parental consciousness, on the other hand, could probably not coexist with the maternal instinct. It is no more male or female than a community or political consciousness is male or female. The parental consciousness is probably at least as much at work before a child is born as after. The community consciousness of a homeowner the day possession of a home is taken is not developed to the degree that it is when he or she has lived in that home for five years.

The same thing could be said for a parent about the day a baby is born. As the child grows and develops and the parent feels that he or she is part of that growth and development, so does the parental consciousness emerge.

All too often, the parental consciousness becomes confused with the parental ego. The unfortunate reality in many custody battles is that too often two unfit parents are fighting for custody of the children. While, in the upper income brackets, custody of the children means custody of the income, in most custody battles it is the parental ego that is at stake. Parents do not necessarily wait for a divorce to try to establish themselves as the favorite or the "good guy" in the eyes of the children. It has been the bane of many fathers fighting for custody that their former wives have told them that they frankly did not want the children but feared community disapproval and the loss of status which they felt they might undergo had they been accused of lacking a "maternal instinct."

The fathers we have seen who manage most successfully in the full-custody situation are characterized by one of two circumstances: They had either taken prime responsibility in home and child care during the marriage, or they had a highly developed coping mechanism and a deeper desire for challenge than for security. In the latter category, most of the men compared obtaining full custody with a job promotion, calling it, basically, a question of organization. One father, a research chemist who has gained prominence in his field, expressed the opinion that he couldn't understand why the women's movement regarded child-raising as boring and mind-deadening. "It's been the most challenging and rewarding experience of my life," he told us.

It is undoubtedly true that many men fighting for custody are doing so more for the parental ego than the parental consciousness. The thought of a child calling another man "Daddy" can create stirrings of fatherly concern that never existed when the child called him "Daddy." A leader of a divorced men's rap group told us, "A lot of guys come to us right after the divorce with a hysterical, melodramatic 'What about my relationship with my children?' Sometimes we have to point out to them that they never had that much of a relationship with their children."

The stereotype of the divorced father whose prime interest is to get out of every financial obligation, with or without seeing his children, does exist in reality. Just as stereotypes of whining, demanding women do exist. The divorced fathers' movement is not trying to deny the existence of this father, nor are they attempting to blame his irresponsibility and incompetence on a matriarchal system. Nor are they taking the stand that reversing the antifather discrimination practices now prevalent is going to give every father, married or divorced, an instant parental consciousness.

But more factors are at work than a divorced or divorcing father suddenly being hit with a sentimental attack of some sort of paternal instinct. The raised feminist consciousness, especially when it equates education or the piling up of degrees with an innate superiority to child-raising, does have an effect in raising the parental consciousness in men. Many custodial and custodial-desirous fathers have told us that, given their "druthers," they would have preferred it had their wives been either willing or competent to assume custody. These men have not asked themselves if they would find fulfillment in the parental role. They are simply men who see no other option for their children's stable, secure home environment, even if a few multicolored socks get into the washing machine with the white towels.

Pointing to a steadily increasing divorce rate does not give the full story in the custody picture. The climbing divorce rate is accompanied by a rising rate of dissatisfaction with the child-care role in women. Unfortunately, it sometimes takes the birth of two or more children for some women to realize that motherhood is "not their bag."

The parental consciousness will have to be raised among more than just divorced fathers. Many divorced mothers may find that their parental consciousness will be raised only at the expense of the maternal instinct, and they are not giving up all that easily. School officials and doctors will have to realize that a father who wants to find out about his children's health and education progress is not to be treated as an imposter. Relatives of the divorced, noncustodial father will have to become aware of their responsibility in making the children aware that not only do they have two parents, but they are the products of two families as well. The judicial system will have to come to terms with the fact that what now passes for "the best interests of the child" is, in fact, the best interests of the lawyers representing the parents in a custody battle. Community and civic organizations will have to provide homemaking and child-care training courses for the single father.

It would be entirely too simplistic to attribute either the rising divorce rate or the lowered interest in child care to the women's movement. Today, no one can speak of the movement without asking, "Which women's movement?" We all know that there are factions of the women's movement that are against marriage and child-raising. But there are other factions that are interested in improving the quality of life for children as well as adults. Among these are women who feel that working outside the home will result in an improved parental consciousness on the part of mothers, as well as providing the child with a fully developed human being for a mother, rather than a household drudge. These are the women who feel that men should not be cheated out of their parental role any more than women should be cheated out of their participation in the work force. We must realize that a raised parental consciousness on the part of women will lead to improved father–child interaction, either during or after a marriage.

Unfortunately, one category of women whose parental consciousness is raised at least as high as her humanitarian consciousness is the category most denounced and vilified by the self-righteous moralists—the woman who realizes that one or more of her children may thrive better in her former husband's custody than in her own. It would be too easy to regard the custody-relinquishing mother as combination jet-setter, Messalina, and female corporate magnet. Such a mutation, if it were to exist, would probably fight for custody. It should also be remembered that many mothers who now have custody of young children have agreements with their former husbands that custody arrangements can change according to the changing needs of the children. There are at least as many noncustodial mothers who maintain a close, open, and flexible visitation relationship with their children as there are noncustodial fathers. It is unfortunate that these women, whose parental consciousness surpasses their parental ego, are still looked upon with disapproval.

Fortunately, we are on the threshold of progress in the areas of postdivorce adjustment for both fathers and children. A fathering study, funded by the Rockefeller Foundation, is being conducted by Dr. Harry Finkelstein Keshet at Brandeis University. Dr. Keshet is to be credited for his studies on the developing and heightened parental consciousness on the part of divorced fathers. Similar studies are being conducted in other major universities, although most of them are still in the embryonic stage. At this writing, plans are being drawn up for a National Center for Child Custody Information. Their goals include producing studies on the sociopsychological acceptability of the father as sole-custodial and joint-custodial parent as a viable alternative to current custody practices; producing a "how-to" pamphlet for attorneys for paternal or joint-custody suits; compiling and making available a list of consultants and expert witnesses in the fields of family law, medicine, psychiatry, and social work; filing *amicus curiae* briefs advocating equal rights for parents as well as children; and enlisting media aid to lobby for vital legislation, both local and federal, prohibiting, for example, interstate "kidnapping." It is also interesting to note that one of the aims of the center is to lobby against national advertising campaigns in the media depicting the father as incompetent homemaker.

One important area where the parental consciousness will have to be raised is among childless women who form relationships with divorced fathers. Unless the couple agrees to keep their relationship separate from his involvement with the children, the woman will find herself having to take some responsibility for children who are not her own.

When the parental ego replaces the parental consciousness, children are used as pawns at least as often during a marriage as after it. When children are used as pawns in a custody battle, it is highly likely that they were used as pawns during the marriage, and it would be misleading to pinpoint the divorce as placing the children in a pawn position.

Realistic or not, the two-parent home is still equated with emotional security and stability where child-raising is concerned, and the one-parent home, more commonly referred to as the "broken" home, is equated with the absence of this stability and security. The divorce-defensive are trying to reverse these definitions by developing proof that the one-parent home guarantees stability. These arguments have the ring of some members of the homosexual rights movements, who would like to convince us that the only suitable environment for child-raising is the household headed by two practicing homosexuals.

We have visited a number of one-parent homes, both mother- and father-headed. Many custodial mothers played hostess to us in our travels and introduced us to the custodial fathers. We were impressed by the degree of stability displayed by these families. It is our contention that the success of these households is directly attributable to the degree of stability of the parents running them.

To issue a series of nonnegotiable demands that fathers automatically be awarded custody in 50 percent of all divorces instead of the 5 percent they now receive would lead to, at best, a series of legislative victories and humanitarian defeats. Zealous antidiscrimination law enforcement in certain areas of education have resulted in a lowering of standards all around.

Technology has not, as yet, produced a machine that can analyze whether a parent is fighting for custody due to a parental consciousness rather than the parental ego. But we can no longer automatically assume that a man is incompetent to raise children because of his maleness any more than we can assume a woman is competent because of her femaleness. We can no longer refer to "the best interests of the child" when we are, in fact, referring to the best interests of others. We will have to realize that the parental consciousness is not something automatically conferred upon parents either upon the birth of a child or upon a decision to divorce. It is a consciousness that will have to be raised in all of us.

APPENDIX A
DIVORCED FATHERS'
GROUPS

Many of these groups have other chapters within their states. Write for information. Groups offering special services or out-of-state membership will be noted. See chapter 12 for a complete discussion of these services.

ALASKA
Fathers United for Equal Rights
P.O. Box 897
Ward Cove   99928

ARIZONA
United States Divorce Reform
21 E. Adams St.
Phoenix   85026

CALIFORNIA
Fathers for Equal Justice
13822 Bordeaux
Garden Grove   92643

Fathers for Equal Rights
P.O. Box 6327
Albany   94706

In Pro Se, Inc.
P.O. Box 3374
Huntington Park   90255

United States Divorce Reform, Inc.
P.O. Box 243
Kenwood   85452

CONNECTICUT
Divorced Men's Association of
      Connecticut
P.O. Box 723
Waterbury   06720
(See Suggested Reading)

DELAWARE
Male Parents for Equal Rights
1 W. 6th St.
Wilmington   19801

Appendix

FLORIDA
National Society of Fathers for
    Child Custody and Divorce
    Law Reform
P.O. Box 010-847
Flagler Station
Miami   33101
(See Suggested Reading and Ap-
    pendix C)

ILLINOIS
American Divorce Association for
    Men (ADAM)
343 So. Dearborn St.
Chicago 60607
(See Appendixes B and C)

United States Divorce Reform
5756 No. Jersey Ave.
Chicago   60659

MAINE
United States Divorce Reform
138 Ocean St.
So. Portland   04106

MARYLAND
Equal Rights in Divorce
P.O. Box 211
Clarksburg   20734

Fathers United for Equal Rights
P.O. Box 9751
Baltimore   21204

MASSACHUSETTS
Fathers United for Equal Justice
2 Brewer St.
Cambridge   02138

Fathers United for Equal Justice
P.O. Box 8428
Boston   02114

MICHIGAN
Council on Family Law Reform in
    Michigan
106 E. Mill St.
Copac   48014

MINNESOTA
Divorce Education Association
3935 Upton Ave. So.
Minneapolis   55410

United States Divorce Reform
2909 Nicholas Ave.
Minneapolis   55468

NEW HAMPSHIRE
Fathers United for Equal Justice
17 Ministrial Rd.
Bedford   03102

Fathers United for Equal Justice
2500 No. River Rd.
Manchester   03104

NEW JERSEY
Fathers United for Equal Rights
P.O. Box 217
Fair Lawn   07410

NEW YORK
Equal Rights for Fathers of New
    York State
Leader Box 969
Corning   14830

Fathers United for Equal Rights
30 Rockefeller Plaza
Suite 3315
New York   10020

OHIO
Ohio Divorce Reform Inc.
P.O. Box 331
Willoughby   44094

OKLAHOMA
Fathers for Fairness
8127 E. 16th St.
Tulsa   74112

PENNSYLVANIA
Family Law Reform and Justice
    Council
P.O. Box 60
Broomal   19008
(Maintains list of individuals na-
    tionwide interested in form-
    ing groups)

RHODE ISLAND
Fathers United for Equal Justice
128 Pocasset Ave.
Providence   02909

Fathers United for Equal Justice
48 Campbell Ave.
Rumford   02914

TEXAS
Texas Fathers for Equal Rights
P.O. Box 50052
Dallas   75250

Texas Fathers for Equal Rights
2514 W. Mulberry
San Antonio   78228

WASHINGTON
United States Divorce Reform
P.O. Box 11
Auburn   98002

WISCONSIN
Wisconsin Institute on Divorce
P.O. Box 1905
Milwaukee   53201
(Publishes recommended news-
    letter)

Divorce Reform, Inc.
P.O. Box 262
Somerset   54025

CANADA
Canadian Fathers Association
Suite 105, 2040 Cornwall St.
Vancouver 9, B.C.

Society of Single Fathers
415-70 Clipper Rd.
Willowdale, M2J 4E3, Ontario

**Note: The following are special-
    interest groups:**

Children's League of Divorced
    Parents
P.O.Box 9751
Baltimore, Md.   21204

Children's Rights, Inc.
3443 17th St. N.W.
Washington, D.C. 20010
(National)

Missouri Council on Family Law
P.O. Box 104
Foley, Mo.   63347
(Specializes in child retrieval; see
    chapter 11)

United Parents of Absconded
    Children
Box 127-A Wolf Run Rd.
Cuba, N.Y.   14727
(Specializes in child retrieval; see
    chapter 11)

Appendix

Many divorced fathers' groups welcome female membership. The following have auxiliary women's organizations:

Second Wives Coalition, Inc.
P.O. Box 9751
Baltimore, Md.   21204

Second Wives Coalition
P.O. Box 42
Fords, N.J.   08863

APPENDIX B
SINGLE-PARENT
AND CHILD-HELP GROUPS

Center for Children in Family
    Crisis
1603 Arrott Bldg.
401 Wood St.
Pittsburgh, Pa.   15222

    For parents and children, focus
    on changes from divorce.

Children Facing Divorce
Evergreen Developmental Center
Denver, Colo.

    Videotape equipment, rap
    groups. Dr. Kenneth Magid,
    director of the program, em-
    phasizes, "It is not
    psychotherapy."

Children of Divorce Project
University of California
Berkeley, Calif.

    This is the Wallerstein and
    Kelly project (see page 102)
    that offers a multifaceted ap-
    proach including rap groups
    for helping children deal
    with their problems. In-

dividual counseling and
group projects for children.

Coping with Family Change
Hennepin County, Dept. of Court
    Services
Minnesota Dept. of Education
Hennepin County, Minn.

    Groups for children; conducted
    in schools.

Creative Growth Workshop
Hunter College
New York, N.Y.

    Created by Elaine Rapp,
    formerly an art and dance
    therapist, now an associate
    professor at Hunter College,
    primarily in order to set up
    an atmosphere where visita-
    tion parents and their
    children may interact mean-
    ingfully. Ms. Rapp trains
    other leaders to set up
    similar programs in their
    areas.

Appendix

Custody Study Institute of
 America
1276 Hopmeadow St.
Simsbury, Conn.   06070

  Evaluation panel for courts.

Dept. of Health Services
Marin Community Mental Health
 Services
250 Bon Air Rd.
P.O. Box 2728
San Rafael, Calif.   94902

  Children of Divorce Project

Divorce Resource and Mediation
 Center, Inc.
14 Story St., Mezzanine
Cambridge, Mass.   02138

  Multifaceted services; parents
  and children. Special
  divorced father programs.
  Described more fully on page
  122.

Evergreen Developmental Center
Dr. Kenneth Magid
Evergreen, Colo.

  Children Facing Divorce Project.

FOR MEN ONLY
YMHA
999 Wilmont Road
Scarsdale, N.Y.   10583

  Rap sessions for men, social
  planning, divorce-law
  reform. Divorced women invited to group once a month.

Jordan, Ms. Lucy
Apt. 12, Lexington House
518 University Drive
State College, Pa.   16801

  Children of Divorce Project.

Peter Kiviloo
40 Gerrard St. E. #2010
Toronto, Ont., Canada

  Teen course on divorce given in
  high schools.

Men as New Singles (MANS)
6 Millbrook Court
Great Neck, N.Y.

  Rap group—men only.
  Described more fully on page
  122.

National Organization to Insure
 Support Enforcement (NOISE)
12 W. 72nd St.
New York, N.Y.   10023

  Evaluation panel.

North American Conference of
 Separated and Divorced
 Catholics
Paulist Community Center
5 Park St.
Boston, Mass.   02108

  Chapters nationwide. Sensitive,
  impressive literature and aid
  available and applicable to
  non-Catholics. Parent-
  oriented. (See additional information on page 121.)

Parents Without Partners, Inc.
7910 Woodmont Ave.
Washington, D.C.   20014

   Chapters nationwide.
     Multifaceted services for
     parents and children.

Remarrieds, Inc.
Box 742
Santa Ana, Calif.   92701

   Chapters nationwide. Based on
     Parents Without Partners for-
     mat.

Seminars for the Separated
Prof. Robert S. Weiss
Harvard Medical School
58 Fernwood Rd.
Boston, Mass.   02115

   Rap groups—combined, men
     and women. (See page 122
     for further information on
     this group.)

Single Family Project
105 E. 22nd St.
New York, N.Y.   10010

   Services for parents and
     children.

SOLO Center
1832 N.E. Broadway
Portland, Oreg.   97232

   Services for parents and
     children.

Stepparents Forum
Westmount
P.O. Box 4002
Montreal H3Z 2X3, Canada

   Ms. Sharyn Sepinwall of this
     organization has instituted a
     rap group program for
     children of divorce. See Sug-
     gested Reading list; request
     November/December 1976
     issue—information on start-
     ing children's rap groups.

APPENDIX C
LEGAL ADVICE REFERRAL

Virtually all divorced fathers' groups give help in fighting *pro se*. Although it is suggested that people contemplating divorce choose a lawyer referred by the Matrimonial Specialist Section of the local American Bar Association, we recommend checking out the lawyer's philosophy and experience on father custody and liberalized visitation before making any definite commitment.

The following organizations specialize in referring lawyers experienced in paternal custody who offer out-of-state consultation services as well as direct representation.

American Divorce Association for Men (ADAM)
343 So. Dearborn St.
Chicago, Ill.   60607

Offers advice on fighting *pro se* in addition to recommending lawyers.

Custody Study Institute of America
1276 Hopmeadow St.
Simsbury, Conn.   06070

Specializes in custody options; i.e., joint custody, split custody, full father custody, as well as changing custody, i.e., children free to change custodial parent in differing age brackets.

National Center for Child Custody Information
167 Centre St.
New Rochelle, N.Y.   10805

Specializes in joint as well as father custody.

Appendix

National Society of Fathers for Child Custody and Divorce Law Reform
P.O. Box 010-847
Flagler Station
Miami, Fla.   33101

Specializes in father custody of "tender-years" children. They have published books written by lawyers for both attorneys and laymen (see Suggested Reading list).

BIBLIOGRAPHY

CHANGING CUSTODIAL TRENDS

Atkin, Edith, and Rubin, Estelle. *Part-Time Father: A Guide for the Divorced Father*. New York: Vanguard Press, 1976.

Baum, Charlotte. "The Best of Both Parents." *New York Times Magazine*, 31 October, 1976.

Berman, Claire. "Father's Day Is Not Just on June 20." *New York Times*, 18 June, 1976.

Dullea, Georgia. "Joint Custody: Is Sharing the Child a Dangerous Idea?" *New York Times*, 24 May, 1976.

—————. "Who Gets Custody of Children: Fathers Now Are Being Heeded." *New York Times*, 14 October, 1975.

"Equal Custodial Time—A Revolutionary Concept." *Family Law Commentator*, 4, No. 4 (July/August, 1975).

Falligant, Cissi. "If Marriage Ends Up in Court, ADAM's There for Advice." *Chicago Suburban Tribune*, 4 August, 1976.

Family Law Reporter, 2 FLR 2688, 17 Aug., 1976.

Family Law Reporter, 1 FLR 2708, 26, Aug., 1975.

"Fathers Seek Right to Custody." UPI, *Star-Ledger*, (Corning, N.Y.) 4 July, 1976.

Jenks, Carolyn. *Guidelines for Self-Help Rap Groups*. Boston. Conference of Separated and Divorced Catholics. ND.

Levine, Jo Ann. "Parents Agree to Joint Custody." *Christian Science Monitor*, 5 May, 1975.

McFadden, Michael, and Mathison, Richard. "The Other Side of the Coin: Single Fathers." In *Momma: The Sourcebook for Single Mothers*, edited by Karol Hope and Nancy Young. New York: Plume Books, 1976.

Molinoff, Daniel D. "After Divorce, Give Them a Father, Too." *Newsday,* (Long Island, N.Y.) 5 October, 1975.

—————. "Father Knows Best." *New York Times,* 24 June, 1975.

Perry, Jean. "Mom Goes Off to Find Herself: Dad Minds the Kids." *New York Daily News,* 1 April, 1975.

Sassower, Doris. "The Legal Profession and Women's Rights," *Rutgers Law Review,* Fall 1970.

—————. "The Role of Lawyers in Women's Liberation," *New York Law Journal,* 30 December, 1970.

—————. "Women, Power and the Law," *ABA Journal,* May 1976.

"Society of Single Fathers." *News Media Information,* Willowdale, Ontario, July 1975.

Van Gelder, Lawrence. "New Custody Customs: In the 'Best Interests' of the Child." *New York Times,* 30 October, 1976.

Van Gelder, Lindsy. "Lesbian Custody: A Tragic Day in Court." *Ms. Magazine,* September 1976.

White, Laura. "New Pattern Emerges for Children of Divorce." *Boston Sunday Herald Advertiser,* 18 July, 1976.

Winter, Edward J. *Fathers Winning Child Custody Litigation: The Father's Child Custody Handbook.* Miami: River Trials Publishing Co., 1976.

—————. *Tactics in Contested Child Custody Litigation.* Miami: River Trails Publishing Co., 1976.

Zalaznik, Patricia. "Co-Parenting." Boston: Conference of Separated and Divorced Catholics.

DIVORCE EXPERIENCE

Berson, Barbara, and Bova, Ben. *Survival Guide for the Suddenly Single.* New York: St. Martin's Press, 1974.

Corry, John. "The Ever-Popular Extra Man Who Comes to Dinner." *New York Times,* 22 November, 1976.

Doppler, George F. *America Needs Total Divorce Reform—Now!* New York: Vantage Press, 1973.

Epstein, Joseph. *Divorced in America.* New York: E. P. Dutton & Co., 1974.

Goode, William J. *Women in Divorce.* New York: Free Press, 1956.

Hunt, Morton M. *The World of the Formerly Married.* New York: McGraw-Hill, 1966.

Kujawa, Kathleen. "Conference Highlights Problems of Divorced." *Divorce,* March–April 1976.

Lake, Alice. "Divorcees: The New Poor." *McCall's,* September 1976.

Martin, Albert. *One Man, Hurt.* New York: Macmillan Publishing Co., 1975.

Metz, Charles V. *Divorce and Custody for Men.* Garden City, N.Y.: Doubleday & Co., 1968.

Ronan, Thomas P. "A Program for Men Facing the Traumas of Marriage's End." *New York Times*, 30 December, 1976.

Sheresky, Norman, and Mannes, Marya. *Uncoupling: The Art of Coming Apart*. New York: Viking Press, 1972.

Singer, Laura J. "Divorce and the Single Life: Divorce as Development." *Journal of Sex & Marital Therapy*, 1, No. 3 (Spring, 1975).

Steiner, Lee R. *Romantic Marriage: The Twentieth Century Illusion*. Philadelphia: Chilton Books, 1963.

Tosches, Nick. "Broken on the Wheel of Sex." *Penthouse*, January 1976.

Taves, Isabella. "Woman Alone: Divorced Mothers Asking for Trouble." *The Western*, (Litchfield, Conn.), 3 September, 1975.

Weiss, Robert S. *Marital Separation*. New York: Basic Books, 1975.

FATHER ROLE

Benton, Myron. "The Paradox of the American Father." In *The Future of the Family*, edited by Louise Kapp Howe. New York: Simon & Schuster, 1972.

Biller, Henry B. *Father, Child and Sex Role: Paternal Determinants of Personality Development*. Lexington, Mass.: Heath, Lexington Books, 1971.

Biller, Henry, and Meredith, Dennis. *Father Power*. New York: David McKay Company, 1974.

Green, Maureen. *Fathering*. New York: McGraw-Hill, 1976.

Herzog, Elizabeth, and Sudia, Cecilia E. "Boys in Fatherless Families." Washington, D.C.: DHEW Publication No. (OCD) 72-73, 1971.

Hochstein, Rollie. "An Interview with Child Psychiatrist Robert Coles." *Family Circle*, November 1973.

Howard, Kenneth. "An Overdose of Mother Love." *Cosmopolitan*, November 1976.

Lynn, David B. *The Father: His Role in Child Development*. Monterey, Calif.: Brooks/Cole Publishing Co., 1974.

Ribble, Margaret A. *The Rights of Infants*. New York: Columbia University Press, 1965.

DIVORCE EFFECT ON CHILDREN

Bartlett, Kay. "Youngsters the Pawns in Custody Snatchings." AP, *World-Herald*, (Omaha, Neb.), 19 September, 1976.

Despert, J. Louise. *Children of Divorce*. Garden City, N.Y.: Doubleday & Co., 1953.

Dowling, Colette: "Liberation Breeds Rotten Kids." *Cosmopolitan*, November 1976.

Goldstein, Joseph; Freud, Anna; and Solnit, Albert J. *Beyond the Best Interests of the Child.* New York: Free Press, 1973.

Grollman, Earl A., ed. *Explaining Divorce to Children.* Boston: Beacon Press, 1969.

Howe, Charles. "Weekend Father." In *The Future of the Family,* edited by Louise Kapp Howe. New York: Simon & Schuster, 1972.

Miller, Judi. "Dating Someone Else's Daddy." *Viva,* January 1977.

Noble, June and William. *The Custody Trap.* New York: Hawthorn Books, 1975.

Parents Are Forever (pamphlet). Washington, D.C.: Parents Without Partners.

Pascoe, Elizabeth Jean. "Helping Children Survive Divorce." *Woman's Day,* August 1976.

Streshinsky, Shirley. "How Divorce Really Affects Children: A Major Report." *Redbook,* September 1976.

"Study Finds Stepchildren Content." AP, *New York Times,* 28 November, 1976.

Wallerstein, Judith S., and Kelly, Joan B. "The Effects of Parental Divorce." *Journal of the American Academy of Child Psychiatry* 14, No. 4 (Autumn, 1975).

CHANGING PARENTAL ROLES

Curtis, Jean. *Working Mothers.* Garden City, N.Y.: Doubleday & Co., 1976.

Fois, Florence. "The Single Father: A Case Study." *Womensweek* (New York), 8 November, 1976.

Klein, Carole. *The Single Parent Experience.* New York: Walker & Company, 1973.

McFadden, Michael. *Bachelor Fatherhood: How to Raise and Enjoy Your Children as a Single Parent.* New York: Walker & Company, 1974.

"The Single Father: A Full-Time Job." *Newsday,* (Long Island, N.Y.) 9 September, 1975.

MEN'S AND WOMEN'S MOVEMENTS

Alison, Pat. "Runaway Sex." *New Dawn,* August 1976.

Bednarik, Karl. *The Male in Crisis.* Translated from German by Helen Sebba. New York: Alfred A. Knopf, 1970.

Benson, Jim. "Men Make Claim to Equal Rights, Too." *Hudson* (N.J.) *Dispatch,* 18 December, 1976.

Bernard, Jessie. *The Future of Marriage.* New York: Bantam Books, 1973.

Court Watcher (Waterbury, Conn.) Vol. 1, No. 9 (November, 1976).

Donnelly, Margarita. "Alternate-Culture Mirror America." In *The Future of the Family,* edited by Louise Kapp Howe. New York: Simon & Schuster, 1972.

Doyle, Richard. *The Rape of the Male.* St. Paul, Minn.: Poor Richard's Press, 1976.

Farrell, Warren. *The Liberated Man: Beyond Masculinity: Freeing Men and Their Relationships with Women.* New York: Random House, 1976.

Feigen Fasteau, Marc. *The Male Machine.* New York: McGraw-Hill, 1974.

Friedan, Betty. "Should You Accept Alimony?" *Harper's Bazaar,* July 1976.

Geng, Veronica. "Requiem for the Women's Movement." *Harper's,* November 1976.

Goldberg, Herb. *The Hazards of Being Male: Surviving the Myth of Masculine Privilege.* New York: Nash Publishing, 1976.

Gornick, Vivian, and Moran, Barbara K., eds. *Woman in Sexist Society: Studies in Power and Powerlessness.* New York: Basic Books, 1971.

Julty, Sam. *Male Sexual Performance.* New York: Dell, 1976.

Kaye, Harvey E. *Male Survival: Masculinity Without Myth.* New York: Grosset & Dunlap, 1974.

Koch, Stephen. "The Guilty Sex: How American Men Became Irrelevant." *Esquire,* July 1975.

Komisar, Lucy. "The Image of Woman in Advertising." In *Woman in Sexist Society,* edited by Urian Gornick and Barbara K. Moran. New York: Basic Books, 1971.

Sklar, Anna. *Runaway Wives.* New York: Coward, McCann & Geoghegan, 1976.

Young, Jane Jaffe. "Why These Park Slope Women Dumped Their Husbands." *Village Voice,* 24 February, 1975.

DIVORCE STATISTICS AND TRENDS

Divorces: Analysis of Changes. United States, 1969. Vital and Health Statistics System, Series 21 No. 22. Washington, D.C.: U.S. Dept. of Health, Education and Welfare.

"For Doctors' Wives, Clouds But No Silver Linings." *New York Times,* 27 October, 1976.

"Household and Family Characteristics, March, 1975." *Current Population Reports, Series P-20, No. 291. Washington, D.C.: U.S. Government Printing Office, 1976.*

Remarriages: United States. Vital and Health Statistics. Series 21 No. 25. Washington, D.C.: U.S. Dept. of Health, Education and Welfare.

Saline, Carol. "Who's for Seconds?" *Philadelphia,* September 1976.

Some Recent Changes in American Families. Current Population Reports. Special Studies, Series P-23, No. 52. U.S. Dept. of Commerce. Washington, D.C.: Bureau of the Census.

SUGGESTED READING

Atkin, Edith, and Rubin, Estelle. *Part-Time Father: A Guide for the Divorced Father*. New York: Vanguard Press, 1976.

Biller, Henry B. *Father, Child and Sex Role: Paternal Determinants of Personality Development*. Lexington, Mass.: Heath, Lexington Books, 1971.

Biller, Henry, and Meredith, Dennis. *Father Power*. New York: David McKay Company, 1974.

Dreikurs, Rudolf. *Children the Challenge*. New York: Hawthorn Books, 1964.

Epstein, Joseph. *Divorced in America*. New York: E. P. Dutton & Co. 1974.

Gardner, Richard A.: *The Boys and Girls Book about Divorce*. New York: Bantam Books, 1970.

George, Victor and Wilding, Paul. *Motherless Families*. London: Routledge and Kegan, 1972.

Goldberg, Herb. *The Hazards of Being Male: Surviving the Myth of Masculine Privilege*. New York: Nash Publishing, 1976.

Green, Maureen. *Fathering*. New York: McGraw-Hill, 1976.

Lynn, David B. *The Father: His Role in Child Development*. Monterey, Calif.: Brooks/Cole Publishing Co., 1974.

Martin, Albert. *One Man, Hurt*. New York: Macmillan Publishing Co., 1975.

Noble, June and William. *The Custody Trap*. New York: Hawthorn Books, 1975.

Ribble, Margaret A. *The Rights of Infants*. 2nd ed. New York: Columbia University Press, 1965.

Weiss, Robert S. *Marital Separation*. New York: Basic Books, 1975.

Suggested Reading

In addition, we would recommend the following, which are available by subscription or mail order:

Court Watcher
Divorced Men's Assn. of Connecticut, Inc.
P.O. Box 723
Waterbury, Conn.   06720

> Published monthly; free to members; $7.50 per year for nonmembers. Regarded highly by lawyers and laymen alike for its astuteness in observing legal sleight-of-hand.

Divorce
Ms. Faerie Kizzire
113 Evergreen Circle
Arlington, Tex.   76011

> Published 10 times per year; $7.00 per year; discount on bulk subscriptions. Published by North American Conference of Separated and Divorced Catholics. Primarily slanted to the special problems of divorced Catholics, this publication features articles of interest to non-Catholics as well.

Marriage, Divorce and the Family Newsletter
P.O. Box 42
Madison Square Station
New York, N.Y.   10010

> Published 8 times a year; $7.00 per year; discount on bulk subscriptions. Excellent coverage of legislative, community, and social trends nationwide.

The Single Parent
7910 Woodmont Ave.
Washington, D.C.   20014

> Published 10 times a year; subscription $2.75 for PWP members; $5.50 for nonmembers.

SOLO Center News
1832 N.E. Broadway
Portland, Oreg.   97232

> Published monthly by SOLO, Portland single-parents' organization; subscription $2.00 per year. Excellent example of what a community-

sponsored center can do for both parents and children; especially low price of services offered.

Stepparents Forum
Westmount, P.O. Box 4002
Montreal, H3Z 2X2, Canada

Published bimonthly; subscription $5.00 per year. Back issues available. Excellent focus on problems of the divorced father; recommended for nonmarrieds as well.

River Trials Publishing Co.
P.O. Box 010847
Flagler Station
Miami, Fla.   33101

Publishes two books on legal aspects of father custody:

Fathers Winning Child Custody Litigation: The Father's Child Custody Handbook. $12.00. For fathers as well as lawyers.

Tactics in Contested Child Custody Litigation. $12.00. For lawyers.

Both written by Edward J. Winter, Esq., an attorney specializing in paternal custody.

INDEX

Index

Index